Speak Like Jesus

To Elizabeth,

Speak like Him -

for Him.

Karen Porter

Other Books by
Karen Porter

I'll Bring the Chocolate: Satisfying a Woman's
Cravings for Friendship and Faith

Get Ready! Practical Ideas to

Prepare You for Ministry

Speak Like Jesus

Presentation Tips from the Master

Karen Porter

Bold Vision Books
PO Box 2011
Friendswood, Texas 77549

©Copyright Karen Porter 2014

ISBN: 978-0615902067

Library of Congress Number 2013952441

Printed in the U.S.A.

BVB - Bold Vision Books
PO Box 2011
Friendswood, Texas 77549

Dedication

To George

Acknowledgments

Florence Littauer has been and continues to be a huge influence in my life. Florence believed in me before I did. She told me the hard truth about mistakes and flaws, all the while convincing me I could do it. Much of what you read in this book will be things I learned from Florence. Now it is so much a part of me that I dare to write it a book, but she is the one who gifted me with the courage to try. Thank you so much dear Florence as you continue to pour into my life.

There are others who have pushed me toward excellence in speaking. Carol Kent, Carole Lewis, Georgia Shaffer, C. McNair Wilson, Ken Davis, Candie Blankman, Craig Valentine, Gerry Wakeland, and so many more. Thank you for your great help - some of you unaware of how much you contributed.

A special thanks to Deb Strubel. You are the best!

Thank you Katie McDivitt. You are so important to me.

Thank you to all the event planners who believed in me and gave me the opportunity to speak.

Thank you to George who always tells me the truth slathered in love and kindness. Life would be empty without you.

Table of Contents

Introduction

Jesus spoke in synagogues, on hillsides, in the streets, and in small groups and large. At times, thousands followed and sat on hillsides to hear His words. He healed sickness, relieved pain, and spoke words of hope for desperate times. He stayed on message and presented with winsomeness and power.

> Jesus went throughout Galilee, teaching in their synagogues, proclaiming the good news of the kingdom, and healing every disease and sickness among the people (Matthew 4:23 NIV).

Jesus dealt with the current problems and issues of the people who heard Him speak, but His emphasis was broader—eternal. He had answers and He knew how to speak the answers to His audiences. As Christ followers, we also have answers, but we must learn to present, to speak, to communicate, and to give out those answers to audiences in an authoritative, powerful, winsome way.

The competition for your audience's attention is strong, so your presentation must be professional and compelling enough to capture people's fleeting attention. From fabulous sporting extravaganzas to hand-held smart phones, people see, hear, and absorb messages in a variety of ways, all while doing other tasks. From live stage productions to IPads and tablets, our audiences are accustomed to slick professional message lines and flashy multimedia. Audiences expect high-definition graphics and creativity. And why shouldn't they? They can receive what they want each day while watching a large flat-screen from their home easy chair.

How can a speaker compete? With a well-prepared and well-executed message of truth – presented as Jesus would if He was here today.

The good news is that you are a unique and interesting individual. God has placed in you a desire to speak, and you have a unique and interesting story to tell. You have a passion and you have experience. You've learned lessons and discovered answers, so now you can help people who are facing similar problems.

This book will give you the tools and techniques to create compelling messages and craft dynamic presentations. When you learn and apply the techniques and use the tips in this book, you will be equipped to prepare powerful presentations, present without notes, tell interesting and meaningful stories, and you'll know what to do on stage—how to use hand movements, body language, voice inflections, humor, and so much more.

This book isn't meant to be the final word on how to speak but it is meant to be a springboard and to whet your appetite to study and learn more. I never stop learning and I hope you won't either.

Throughout the book, you will find this bonus spotlight feature.

When you see this microphone, go to the website http://speaklikejesus.com to find additional information, videos, clips, illustrations, and bonuses about the page you are reading. Then remember to check back often at the website for new information.

Each chapter has a practice section at the end. Don't skip this important "hands-on" application. When you get to chapter 19, spend time developing your spiritual depth and dependence on God.

So let's get busy and learn how to speak—from the Master.

Chapter 1
Do You Have a Point?

Do you have anything to say and does anyone need to hear it?
– Florence Littauer

Every presentation must have a main point. What is the one over-arching point you want to make? What one thought do you want your audience to hear? What one action do you expect your audience to take after they have heard your presentation? The answers to these questions are critical and must be answered before you can build a successful presentation.

Choose One Main Point

Jesus spoke for approximately three years and changed the world forever. He had one main point.

> "The time has come," he said. "The kingdom of God has come near. Repent and believe the good news!" (Mark 1:15 NIV).

His main focus was the kingdom of God. The kingdom is near and to enter it we must repent and believe. No matter where He spoke or who was in His audience or whatever the topic of the day, His main message—His primary underpinning—was the kingdom of God.

All messages must have a central idea, a theme melody that flows throughout the presentation. If you listen carefully to a symphony, the melody or refrain will appear throughout the performance in various forms and sounds, major and minor keys, different tempos and rhythms. Likewise, your main idea must show up in various forms throughout your sermon, presentation, or speech. Your main point should be one powerful point. The main point isn't the title or topic; it is the central theme. You can't cover everything you know in a 30-minute presentation. So choose one main point, make it, and make it powerful. The audiences will not forget it.

Determine what "tweetable" message is in your total presentation. A tweet is only 142 characters. Can you boil your presentation point down to a tweet?

Use Supporting Arguments

As you think about your one main point, find two to four major sub points or facets of that main point. These sub points will be your foundational statements and the strong evidence that supports your main point. Like a bridge with pilings, the main message must have strong supports so it can transport listeners toward understanding and applying the main point. I'll explain more later in this chapter about how to flesh out these sub points. For now, just decide on your main point and several sub points.

You may wonder why having only one main point and a few sub points is important. Have you ever had a presentation go wrong or flat despite your best efforts? Perhaps your mind has gone blank in the middle of your talk. Maybe all the lights and electric suddenly shut off in the middle of your talk but then came back on just as suddenly. A myriad of things can, and do, happen during a presentation. So be ready with an organized message—point and sub points.

Focus Despite Distractions

Someone said, "Your brain begins working on the day you are born and never stops—until you get up to speak in public. Then it quits." Funny words, but truer than we want to believe. It is so easy to get off the central message and follow a trail to another subject—just in time to discover you have used all your time and didn't say the main thing you wanted to say.

One day, an important official begged Jesus to come to his home because the man's daughter was gravely ill. On the way, crowds pushed closer, each person jostling to get a glimpse of the healer. In the midst of this tumult, a woman who had been ill for years was able to reach out and touch the garment Jesus wore. She hoped to receive healing and she did.

Jesus stopped, cared for the woman's needs, and used the occasion to do some impromptu teaching to the crowd. Even with these distractions, however, He stayed on task. He did not forget His main mission of the day—to go to the synagogue leader's home. You too can stay on task.

As you speak, don't take off on a different path. Stay on the bridge. Continue on to complete and substantiate your main point, even if there are distractions.

Create a Memorable Outline

Staying on track with the main point isn't as hard as you might think if you build an outline that both you and your audience can relate to and remember. You can speak your message with power and charm if you keep to your main point and use an outline to keep yourself on track.

The outline techniques your eighth-grade English teacher taught—you remember, Roman numeral *I* followed by capital *A* followed by numeric *1* followed by small *a*—are not helpful when you speak. What you need, instead, is a framework to build your message upon—a skeleton where you can hang the flesh of your message. And that framework must be simple, interesting, and easily remembered, especially while you are on stage.

One of the best compliments you can receive as a speaker is for someone in your audience to repeat your outline back to you. The outline in one of my presentations is "Attitude, Gratitude, Certitude." The rhyming outline is easy to remember, and I usually repeat it several times throughout the message. For example, "Not only do you need a great attitude, but you also need to be filled with gratitude." And "Attitude and gratitude aren't all you need; one

15

more thing will make life a success, and that thing is certitude." The audience picks up on the rhyme and the rhythm of the words, and when someone comes to me after the presentation and repeats the outline, I consider the day a great success.

Learn to connect the points of the outline without using numbers.

Jesus used outlines brilliantly.

> Ask and it will be given to you; seek and you will find; knock and the door will be opened to you (Matthew 7:7 NIV).

Notice His framework:

Ask

Seek

Knock

His outline is simple, clear, and easily remembered.

One of my favorite outlines came from superstar singer Reba McIntyre who spoke about living life to the full. She said we need, a "Back Bone, a Funny Bone, and a Wish Bone."

Developing clever outlines that you can remember isn't hard, but you need to understand the different types of outlines in order to build the most successful one. Let's look at a few.

- Rhyme—Choose resonating words or echoing sounds.

Renew

Review

Pursue

****

Imply

Apply

Retry

****

Alive

Survive

Revive

Simply

Deeply

Freely

- Action Verbs—Help your audience achieve a goal or give them instructions.

    Read the Bible

    Pray Aloud

****

Answer harsh words kindly

Offer sympathy freely

Give advice thoughtfully

****

Trust

Obey

- Alliteration—Begin each point in the outline with the same letter.

    Pray

    Ponder

    Proclaim

****

Attend a conference

Accept constructive criticism

Avoid confusing comments

****

Maximization

Motivation

- Questions—Use an inquiry to address a problem or obtain a response.

> What will you do today?
>
> What will you do tomorrow?

****

> Does God care how we speak?
>
> Do people care what we say?
>
> Do we care what words we utter?

- Sentences—Use whole thoughts expressed with noun, verb, and phrases. These outlines are often combined with alliteration, repetition, or rhyming.

> God's love is unmerited
>
> God's love is unconditional
>
> God's love is unending

****

> Choose a time of day
>
> Find a place of quiet
>
> Discover the joy of listening

****

> Why we eat unhealthy foods
>
> Why we don't eat healthy foods
>
> Why we should eat healthy foods

- Acrostics—Choose a central word of the speech and use the first letter to form the outline.

> H—Helping others with our hands
>
> O—Offering peace with our words
>
> P—Placing trust with our minds
>
> E—Extending faith with our hearts

J—Jealousy removed

O—Offenses forgiven

Y—Youthfulness restored

- Pictures or other visuals—Use one visual to depict the outline.

A photo of a tree would allow you to use the parts of the tree as your outline:

Fruit

Leaves

Limbs

Trunk

Roots

A photo of a mountain would allow you to use mountain climbing techniques as metaphors for the points in your outline.

Build up your strength

Use the right gear

Climb with a partner

Keep moving

- How to…—Offer techniques to listeners to accomplish a task. Numbers are effective when used in the title of a "How to" topic.

> Three Keys to Building a Prayer Team
> 1. Choose the right people
> 2. Meet regularly
> 3. Learn prayer tools

****

> Four Ways to Build a Speech
> 1. Determine the main point
> 2. Structure an outline
> 3. Add illustrations and examples
> 4. Enhance with sources

- Chart—Use a diagram or map to direct the audience's attention.

Instead of listing the points, use a photo of stair steps to teach the steps to stronger faith.

A diagram of the body would be an interesting way to outline 1 John 1:1:

Ears: We have heard. Eyes: We have seen. Hands: We have touched.

- Lists—Prepare a list of thoughts or actions to motivate your audience.

    Faith is taking the first step when you can't see the way.

    Faith is being sure that God is in control.

    Faith is placing your future in God's hands.

- Comparison/Contrast—Use similar or contradictory objects or terms to prove your main theme.

    Live Healthy/Live Happy

    Eat Veggies/Shun Sugar

- Scripture—Let the words in the verses form the outline.

    Galatians 1:3

    Grace and Peace – from God to you

    ****

    Psalm 146:5

    Help and Hope

    ****

    Psalm 84:11

    Sun and Shield

Use Parallelism in Outlines

As you develop your outlines, learn to make the outline parts match. If you choose to use a sentence style, all points in the outline should be sentences, and the sentences should have the same structure. This is called parallelism. Consider this example:

    Peace is possible when all parties negotiate with compromise.

    Putting fresh ideas on the table helps promote peace.

Both of these outline statements are sentences, but the sentences don't match in form or format. The outline above will be difficult to remember and articulate. Changing the order of the words in the second point will help both the speaker and the hearer remember the outline. Here is a better outline:

> Peace is possible when all parties negotiate with compromise.

> Peace is promoted when all parties put fresh ideas on the table.

If the outline consists of single words, each word should be the same part of speech. For example, a presentation on how to keep up with family schedules might have a single-word outline like this:

> Clock

> Calendar

> Coordinate

The outline looks good on the surface. The words are clear and all begin with the same letter. On closer inspection, however, we see these words are not the same part of speech. Clock and calendar are nouns. They describe objects. Coordinate is a verb, which describes an action. So the three words don't really go together. They are not parallel. The outline can be improved by changing the last item to a noun.

> Clock

> Calendar

> Coordination

Now the outline works. A speaker could put this three-point outline into his or her mind and stand before a crowd and give a presentation without any notes. If you know the outline and can add a story or two and some facts and information for each point, the presentation suddenly becomes full and stimulating for the audience. As an added plus, if you have distractions during your presentation, you as the speaker are not as at risk of forgetting what you planned to say.

The most important aspect of an outline is whether you can remember it on stage or not. Simple outlines are easier to bring to mind. If you write long, involved sentences for your outline, you will likely need to read the points. You won't remember the outline and neither will your audience.

Include Good Illustrations

As you flesh out each point in your outline, use illustrations to make each concept clearer. Metaphors, word pictures, and stories communicate better than information, advice, or lectures. Personal stories are the best source for illustrations. Far better than canned or memorized stories, your personal stories will enhance your persona before the crowd. Such stories will be the most interesting ones because you were there. You will be able to add emotion, act out portions, or extract details for particular audiences because you know the story intimately. As an added bonus, you don't need to memorize a personal story; you know what happened.

A clever story, an entertaining illustration, or an amusing example keeps your message interesting but should never sidetrack or confuse your audience. Make the point and use an illustration to support it and not to distract. Sometimes you'll need to remove extraneous details from the story or portions of the ending so your audience can focus on your main point.

Other ways to make your presentations more interesting are to use props and media. We will discuss all these later in the book. The most important feature of an illustration, media, or prop is that it must enhance the point of the presentation. It must never distract in any way.

Add Supportive Authority

Another way to strengthen each point is to present some authority behind your statements. There are numerous ways to back up and support what you say. Incorporate statistics, facts, data, numbers, measurements, and evidence into each point to drive home your idea. Quotes from respected sources also strengthen points. Verses from the Bible and quotations from experts will solidify and reinforce your message. Use all these as ways to give your message credibility.

Add Appropriate Applications

Two other powerful techniques will give heft and value to the points in your message. First, explain how the point of the message applies to your hearers. It isn't enough for your audience to hear that they need to forgive unless you show through illustration and authoritative evidence how the act of forgiveness can change relationships and situations. When your listeners gain a glimpse of how the point might fit into their lives, you have a successful presentation. Second, give your audience some specific, definable actions to take. What is the next step each person should take and when and how should he or she take it? Be as detailed and precise as possible as you give these instructions. List the activities, arrangements, and deeds that will lead to success.

Remember the Formula

A speech must have one over-arching point. Strong sub points called an outline should support that theme. An outline must be clear, concise, and easy for both the speaker and the audience to remember. Each point must have an illustration or two (the best are personal stories), an authority behind it (quotes or verses or facts and expert opinions), an application, and action steps to take.

Great Presentation Formula

Theme

+

Clear Outline

+

Illustrations

+

Authority

+

Application

+

Action steps

=

Great Presentation

Practice

1. Write a three-point outline about healthy living.

2. Using Psalm 145:8 as your text, prepare an outline using one of the types of outlines discussed in this chapter. Then redo the outline, putting it into each of the other outline formats.

3. Review a presentation you have already prepared or perhaps already given. Does it have all the elements of the Great Presentation Formula?

Chapter 2
Speak with Authority

Every speaker/presenter needs to know their material. I don't mean their lines; I mean their subject matter and the objective of their talk.

—Curtis O. Fletcher

Jesus spoke with authority. His words were solid and strong. He never beat around the bush as He convinced and persuaded His hearers. In contrast, the religious leaders of His day taught the Scriptures with wavering, qualifying statements. They taught what they had been taught, referring to other teachers, not God, as the authority. These religious teachers also added new rules (the Talmud) because they weren't sure of God's law or perhaps didn't like what they feared God's law was saying. When Jesus came on the scene, He spoke as One who had great knowledge and confidence. He knew God's law intimately. He also knew all the background and culture surrounding the law so His teaching was robust, weighty, and authoritative.

> One day He entered the synagogue at Capernaum.
> Then they went into Capernaum, and immediately on the Sabbath He entered the synagogue and taught. And they were astonished at His teaching, for He taught them as one having authority, and not as the scribes (Mark 1:21-22 NKJV).

A typical synagogue service consisted of prayer, praise, the reading of the Word of God, and an exposition by any rabbi or other competent person in attendance. When Jesus arrived, they recognized Him as a traveling teacher and invited Him to speak. He surprised the people because He taught with authority. The word *astonished* means "shocked or struck with panic." Like a lightning bolt, these people knew they were hearing a new, different, confident, reliable voice. Jesus' authority in teaching the Word correctly came from God. In his commentary, K. S. Wuest said, "The rabbis quoted from other rabbis and felt themselves to be expounders of tradition. The Messiah struck a new note here, and the people were quick to recognize it. They saw that here was a Teacher who spoke on His own authority."[i]

Yes, Jesus was God, so He could speak with authority like no other person who had ever lived; you and I aren't Jesus, but we can speak with authority. I've heard too many speakers who stand before a crowd and belittle themselves by saying, "I'm not the expert." Other speakers apologize for not having time to really study or for some other supposed weakness. Even speakers who couch their words in weak language by using qualifying words like *probably* or *seemingly* or *apparently* cause their whole presentation to sound feeble, frail, and pathetic. Never apologize or equivocate about your subject matter. Be sure and strong, not evasive and unsure.

Study for Confidence

For Christians, confidence is found by studying in several key areas.

1. Know God. Spend time with God and be sure that you know Him, His character, and His ways. When you know Him well, you will be able to cast a vision to others that will help them know Him, too.

2. Know your material. Prepare, prepare, prepare. You will likely need to study and work on your presentation about two to five hours for each ten minutes of the presentation time. You will become an expert on your topic. You will learn so much more than you will have time to communicate to your audience, but this knowledge will give you confidence. It will also add power to your presentation.

    I once taught a four-week course on angels in the Bible. As I started preparing for these presentations, I realized I needed to know more about angel appearances in Scripture. I spent hours and hours reading every verse in the Bible that referred to an angel. I not only read those verses, I hand-wrote each verse into a spiral notebook—old school. By the time I finished, I had a broad personal knowledge and awareness of all the biblical incidents of angels. Then, I was able to organize the material into the four-week course. As the course continued, curious students asked questions about angels—questions I had not anticipated—but because I had been so thorough in my research, I had answers.

3. Learn about topics that relate to or surround your topic. Study about things that touch on or influence your topic. You may learn about the culture or the dress of the time period you speak about. You may learn some interesting facts about concepts or theories. You can't use all this information because your presentation time is limited, but that doesn't mean your efforts will be wasted. Since you have all this information and background packed into your mind, your presentation will take on a richer and more powerful tone.

4. Believe your material. Don't speak on a subject unless you are totally sold on the concept, facts, and certainty of the material. If it is a theological truth, have you embraced the reality of it? If it is an action step, are you willing to make the first move? When you believe what you speak, power and authority fill your presentation.

5. Use the best words. Use strong verbs and colorful descriptions to make your presentation as interesting and powerful as it can be. Convince your hearers with the best images and metaphors. Persuade your audience with compelling language. Check this list of strong verbs at http://speaklikeJesus.com

Answer with Scripture

When Jesus was trapped in the wilderness, tired and hungry, He countered the threats and temptations of Satan with verses of Scripture. You have this powerful tool available too. Satan offered food, but Jesus said there is greater satisfaction than food by quoting from Deuteronomy 8:3: "Man shall not live by bread alone." Satan offered fame and celebrity status, but Jesus quoted Deuteronomy 6:13: "You must worship the Lord your God and serve only Him." Satan tried to get Jesus to use His powers for the spectacular, saying, "Throw yourself off this temple and the angels will catch you." Jesus answered with another Scripture: "You must not test the Lord your God" (Deuteronomy 6:16).

God's Word is powerful and alive. (See Ephesians 6:17; Hebrews 4:12.) Read the Bible and memorize verses or portions of it. Then you can use it like a powerful sword to counteract the attacks of the enemy. Did you know verses could be wielded like swords? The Bible calls itself the sword of the Spirit, sharper than a double-edged sword.

Incorporate the Five Senses

When John wrote his letters, he spoke to fellow Christians with the authority of an eyewitness.

> We proclaim to you the one who existed
> from the beginning, whom we have heard
> and seen. We saw him with our own eyes
> and touched him with our own hands. He
> is the Word of life (1 John 1:1 NLT).

Did you notice how John used the senses to illuminate the whole truth? The five senses are a great way to make your message clear. Describe how whatever you are referring to feels, how it sounds, how it smells, what it looks like, and even how it tastes. Your messages will become even stronger.

Practice carefully watching the things around you. You will be able to tell better stories, making them more believable and captivating since you will be able to use the five senses. When you use the five senses, you transport your audience to the spot, and as you hear, see, look, and touch the surroundings, they will too.

If I used a hospital waiting room as an example of how different people face a crisis, then I could describe the room as dull, quiet, and as having various people waiting in different ways. Then I could challenge the audience to face whatever crisis comes along with patience and faith. You would get the idea, but it wouldn't be an exciting, memorable presentation. If I want you to enter the story and *really* understand my point, I might tell you about a hospital waiting room like this:

> Surrounded by gray walls and dingy carpet, I sat on the fake leather straight-back chair. I stared at the cheap prints framed in plastic, hanging slightly askew on the wall in front of me. Across the room, a tall, lanky cowboy tapped his boot and twisted the edge of his big hat. He never looked up and seemed to be muttering to himself. Perhaps he was praying. Behind him on the other side of the row of chairs, a man in a business suit looked like a caged animal as he paced back and forth, all while typing furiously into his Blackberry. On my right was an elderly woman in a wheelchair crying softly into a tissue. The aroma of fresh coffee filled the room as her granddaughter brought a paper cup to the woman and whispered words of comfort.
>
> The scene is a snapshot of how we wait. Patiently anticipating the next news and perhaps whispering prayers like the cowboy. Trying to take care of business and maintain control of some things like the businessman. Maybe crying without hope like the grandmother or bringing comfort to those who hurt like the granddaughter.

Using the senses to describe the scene makes the story come alive, and your points will be strong and memorable.

Condense for Clarity

Be careful as you use detailed descriptions of events to make your point. Too many details will bore your audience and get them sidetracked. Gerry Wakeland, president of CLASSeminars, tells a great story that illustrates how the life of a traveling speaker isn't all glamour and fun. This true story is so funny, but it covers about two weeks of travel and event mishaps. Telling the full story can take nearly thirty minutes, but a long detailed story loses the audience and the point. We spent hours pulling out the main points and the most interesting details, so that she can tell the story in one to three minutes. The story is still funny, but now the points are more compelling and interesting.

Your challenge is to edit your story to include succinct, captivating descriptions that fascinate your audience and convince them of your point or the action you want them to take.

In his book *The Preacher: His Life and World*, J. H. Howett said, "I have a conviction that no sermon is ready for preaching, not ready for writing out, until we can express its theme in a short, pregnant sentence as clear as crystal." After you've done the work to develop your one main point and give it a supporting outline and flesh it out with stories and authority, then condense it to one sentence. Until you can do this with the presentation, you are not ready to give it.

Authority and Confidence

Be so well prepared that you will be able to give your presentation with power and confidence. Use Scripture as your plumb line and the five senses as your viewpoint. Condense the stories and points to make them stronger.

Practice

1. Review the five steps to confidence on pages 28 and 29. Determine which one is your strongest. Why? Which one is your weakest? What can you do to strengthen this area of your presentation?

2. Write a true story using all five senses. Now cut the word count by one-half and rewrite the story.

3. Using a presentation you've already given or one you are working on, write a strong, crystal-clear sentence describing the theme.

Chapter 3
Be Current and Relevant

Any subject can be made interesting and any subject can be made boring.

--Unknown

In Matthew chapters 5 and 6, Jesus addresses real issues of His audience. In chapter 5, He tackles tough subjects such as anger (verses 21-26), lust (verses 27-30), divorce (verses 31-32), oaths (verses 33-37), retaliation (verses 38-42), and enemies (verses 43-48). In chapter 6, He concentrates on giving to the needy (verses 1-4), learning to pray (verse 5-15), and fasting (verses 16-18).

It would have been easier for Jesus to speak about less harsh ideas. He could have taken up the cause of the zealots who wanted freedom from Roman domination. He could have used the same techniques as the rabbis who used quotes from previous teachers without causing controversy. And He could have tried to please the crowds who wanted to see His miracles and eat the bounty when He gave out food from a boy's lunch. Any of these topics would have been easier, more popular, and less invasive into the lives of the hearers.

Instead, Jesus went to the core of life. His messages confronted the inner thoughts. People should not live with anger or let lust overtake their hearts. Commitments, such as marriage, promises, and contracts, were not to be entered into frivolously and were to be honored. He challenged people to give generously and care for the needy.

Jesus spoke about real-life issues and topics the hearers needed to hear. He spoke about current issues and concepts. He dug down to the roots of personal problems, and He challenged the people to do more than the minimum in their relationships.

Don't Use Fluff

As speakers, we need to be up-to-date. Don't speak fluff and tell useless stories—no matter how entertaining they might be or how much you like the story. People are hurting. People need answers. Speakers who adopt deep, spiritual certainty as the basis of each presentation are able to speak significant, beneficial truth.

A few years ago, I began to feel the need for more depth and wisdom in my presentations as I traveled the country speaking to hundreds of women's church groups. I had written a book titled *I'll Bring the Chocolate*, which compared all the luscious qualities of women's friendships to all the luscious qualities of chocolate.

Many of the events related to the book are elaborate girls-night-out-chocolate parties. The attendees come for a night of relaxation and the party gives the women an opportunity to get away from the stress of jobs and responsibility and for an hour or so, laugh and relax. I have developed several presentations that are full of humorous stories and give the audience just what they expect—a lot of fun. The events are a huge success. I enjoy myself at these events and, frankly, it is invigorating to hear the crowds laugh as I present my humor. Okay, I'll admit it, I've even felt a bit of pride that I can be so entertaining. It is easy for me to get caught up in the excitement.

One morning, after weeks of successful events, I sat in my favorite chair to read my Bible. As I meditated on the passage and prayed, I sensed God's reprimand. "Karen, I didn't call you to be a comedienne." Yes, God made me funny, but He didn't intend my presentations to be shallow or fluffy. My calling is to present relevant truth that changes hearts and behaviors and points to Jesus. I can fulfill my purpose in a pleasant, even a funny way, but being funny isn't my primary role.

Although the book *I'll Bring the Chocolate* is full of fun stories and chocolate recipes, it also contains rich spiritual truths about faith, loyalty, forgiveness, and encouragement. When I speak in a retreat setting and have three or four sessions to delve into these concepts deeply, I like to help the women understand deep spiritual concepts. But the one-talk, girls-night-out events fell short of my true calling. So now I'm careful to include the richer, deeper concepts along with the fun.

Stay Current

Stay up to date on the news. Before you go on stage, be sure you have read today's newspaper or an online news source. Be aware of recent tragedies, world crisis events, big sports news, and even celebrity news. You may or may not use the news in your presentation, but being unaware of it could be disastrous. Also, check out the local news for the community or city where you are speaking. Being uninformed about a local tragedy such as a car accident involving local high school kids could be embarrassing or awkward, and you could miss a ministry opportunity.

Being current also means being aware of the latest in technology and social media. I encourage you to participate in social media opportunities. These platform-building tools are an excellent way to connect with and influence people. Even if you don't want to participate in social media, know what it is, how it works, and never belittle those who do participate.

Using illustrations that happened recently will build the audience's confidence. Telling how God intervened in your life years ago or how your trusted Him when you were a teen will leave your audience wondering, "What has God done for you lately?" If you tell old stories, be sure to also tell current fresh events, too.

Jesus not only spoke about real-life issues, He responded to the needs of the people around Him. In Matthew 8:14-15, He visited Peter's home. Upon arrival, Jesus and His disciples discovered Peter's mother-in-law was ill. Jesus healed her. She got up from her sick bed and served them. Although we don't have the power of Jesus to raise someone from his or her sick bed with a simple word or touch, we do have the power to speak peace, comfort, and encouragement to those who are ill or hurting.

Be Relevant

At the end of every event, folks will wait in line to speak with me or to tell me about a difficult situation in their lives. It may be physical illness or family difficulties or personal tragedy. My response must be relevant and kind. Though I'm not a professional counselor, a practicing physician, or a psychologist, I have options when dealing with a distressed person.

First, I listen carefully and attentively. Talking to someone who listens may be the healing balm the person needs. A kind and encouraging response could be all the person wants. Praying for the person on the spot is often curative and restores hope. If I sense a bigger need, then I refer the person to the local doctors, pastors, or counselors rather than offering medical or psychological advice. I usually discuss this concept with the event planner ahead of time and ask that he or she have a qualified person standing by.

Be Salt and Light

Jesus commanded us to be salt and light in the world (see Matthew 5:14). As salt, we flavor the world around us with truth and encouragement. Salt also preserves. Speaking the message of Jesus offers hope and healing to audiences. Your choice of subject matter and your compelling presentation skills may rescue or revive a person's life. Just as light brings out things hidden in the dark, your presentation may bring awareness and insight to darkened minds.

Be Real

I received a message from a writer friend who is writing about some of the events of his life. He said, "The story is more about failures than success—far more." I can't wait to read his story because I know it will be real. My husband and I teach a First Place 4 Health wellness class each week at our church. We are all trying to eat healthy foods, exercise regularly, and study the Bible, inviting God in on the journey of being obedient with our bodies. When my class understood that I failed on the journey during the past week, they saw me as a real and authentic person. I am on the journey with them, and they take encouragement from the idea that when we fail, we can start again.

Don't stand before your audience as the perfect Christian or even give the impression that you have figured everything out and you never make a mistake or take a step backward. If you talk about success after success, they won't believe you or relate to you. Neither will they apply the message—unless they know you have also experienced the failures and setbacks along with success. Don't be afraid of your flaws and disappointments. They will relate if you are similar to them.

Be Fresh

I heard one of America's most talented and well-known speakers present her most requested presentation. Though I had heard this presentation numerous times, and she has spoken it thousands of times, she gave the message and the illustrations with joy, enthusiasm, and a freshness that thrilled the audience and caused us all to marvel. We must keep our messages crisp, fresh, and full of energy and passion. We can stay fresh by first staying current with God through daily time with Him learning more about Him and His character and attributes.

Second, we need to stay (or get) physically healthy. Exercise will make you strong and healthy. Eating healthy foods will build your stamina for the long hours of travel in uncomfortable airplanes and enhance your energy, endurance, and resilience.

Third, build your message with fresh, passionate, lively words, eliminating clichés and tired religious words. Some "spiritual language" is so tired and old that we have become experts at saying almost nothing. Avoid overused words that are peculiar to the Christian faith. Consider fresh ways to say some of the most common Christian phrases.

Instead of "spoke to my heart," consider something like, "God helped me think a God-thought."

Instead of word of prayer," consider "Let's talk to God."

Instead of "sorely tempted," consider "lured by sin."

Current and Relevant

Choose current, relevant, applicable topics as you prepare your presentations. Consider how you can make the message more germane to the audience. Every story in your presentation must be fresh and make the point. Read and watch the news to stay up to date. Share the hope and healing of Jesus' words with your audience and in one-on-one conversations.

Practice

1. Review your most recent presentation. What specific areas were relevant to the audience?

2. Study every story in your presentation. Is it current? Is it relevant? Does it clearly make your point? If it is from a long time ago, does it ring true now?

3. Fill in the blanks below with some fresh new phrases of your own.

    Instead of "bear fruit," consider _____

    Instead of "carry your cross," consider _____

    Instead of "share a verse," consider _____

    Instead of "walk the talk," consider _____

    Instead of "lead you to the Lord," consider _____

    Instead of "life in prayer," consider _____

Chapter 4
Finding that Sweet Spot

Do you have the gift of speaking? Then speak as though God himself were speaking through you.

1 Peter 4:11 NLT

Like tennis players who connect with the ball using the perfect spot on the racket, or golfers who find the perfect stance and position, speakers can also find the sweet spot. In fact, if you are speaking because you desire to make a difference, to change the world, to draw people to Jesus, or to help people live a fuller life, then you may feel God's anointing when you are fulfilling that purpose.

Definition of Anointing

Anointing is defined as "influence, motivation, inspiration."

Max Lucado said, "When God gives an assignment, He also gives the skills." Your unique abilities, talents, personality, and style put you in the distinctive position of doing what God wants you to do. I often find that when I am on stage in front of a group of people and my presentation is well-prepared, well-ordered, and backed by the truth and principles of Scripture, I feel I am in the sweet spot. I know at that moment I am doing what I'm supposed to be doing and I am standing in the middle of God's will for my life.

While all of us share some stage fright moments, if you shutter and shake and fear the stage, then that might be a sign that speaking isn't for you. Being prepared solves fear and anxiety. Once I get over those first step-on-the-stage butterflies, my fear goes away and my connection with the audience begins.

I think the word *connection* may be more descriptive of this feeling than either *sweet spot* or *anointing*. I like to say connection because an *ah-ha* moment happens when I, the speaker, connect with my audience. If I have prepared my presentation thoroughly and I'm using all the techniques I've learned to present in a powerful and winsome way, then the audience will focus on the message, the Holy Spirit will work, and lives will be changed as audience members take new positive actions.

Factors for Success

Getting that feeling of anointing or hitting the sweet spot is not only determined by preparation and skills but also by three other factors that make each presentation a success: the kind of person you are becoming, your message theme, and what feelings you convey.

The first factor for successful presentations, beyond being in the sweet spot, is the type of person you are becoming. We are all a work in progress. God's primary concern for my life is not who I am or what I've done. His primary concern is who I am becoming. Ask yourself, "Who am I becoming?"

What does success look and feel like to you? If you are unsure, then imagine yourself standing before the gates of heaven where God is assessing your life so far. What one thing do you want God to say about you? Your answer will show you who and what you are in the process of becoming.

For me the answer is that I want to be a person who glorifies God, and to do that in an ongoing way, I need a personal definition of success. To keep myself on track toward my personal definition of success, I ask myself these questions: Am I authentic? Do I really believe what I say I believe? Do I apply the teaching to my life? Do those who know me really know me?

The second factor that goes into successful presentations is your overarching message theme. Ask yourself, "What am I offering?" For me, my overall message theme is hope, so my presentations must have elements of optimism and confidence. I live my life in holy anticipation, expecting God to surprise me each day. I want all my messages to reflect this attitude of hopefulness. Life is an adventure to be faced with courage and faith. If I communicate this potential in my presentations, then I find my sweet spot. Perhaps your message theme is recovery. If so, then your life story, as well as your presentations, should reflect it. If your message is about the power of prayer, then you should be a person of prayer.

The third factor is the feeling you convey through your message, your body language, and your words. Ask yourself, "What emotions will I communicate? Will I leave my audience with guilt, fear, or joy?" I remember hearing a presentation on the dangers of imported meats. I left the meeting afraid to eat a hamburger. The speaker didn't give us any hope or tips on how to choose healthy foods.

I never want a person who has heard me speak to leave the session with apprehension or fear, especially since I speak about spiritual issues and matters of the soul and my message theme is hope. I want to give my audience the opportunity to walk out of the auditorium or event center with an overwhelming feeling of joy. If I do my job well and use the techniques that you'll learn in this book, then I will be able to accomplish my goal.

Feeling God's Smile

What human emotions must have filled John the Baptist! He was preaching truth, he was baptizing converts, he was bringing people to the kingdom…he was doing good things. And people were responding to him and coming to him.

> At this time John the Baptist was baptizing at Aenon, near Salim, because there was plenty of water there; and people kept coming to him for baptism (John 3:23 NLT).

Humanly speaking, we would consider John a successful speaker. He had every reason to feel proud. But he wasn't. He continually turned the audience's eyes and hearts to Christ. He said, "Behold the Lamb." He told the crowds, "I am not the Christ." He counseled his closest disciples, "I must decrease – He [Jesus] must increase!"

When I speak and feel God's smile, it is because I have similar feelings of pointing people to Christ and of keeping the focus off myself. At those times, I sense God is pleased with me. I have prepared. I have learned and practiced the skills. Things are going well. The audience seems to like me. I have much to offer to them, and I feel successful. My dreams are big, but my heart's goal is to shine the light on Jesus. More of Jesus, less of me. There is the sweet spot.

When John heard about all that Jesus was doing, he compared his feeling of seeing Jesus to the joy a bride feels when seeing her bridegroom. John had great joy.

"That joy is mine!" (John 3:29).

The sweet spot for a Christian speaker is when Jesus increases because of what you say. The joy is complete when the words you speak point others to Jesus and not to yourself.

One other aspect of feeling the anointing is when God gives you words that you didn't expect to say. When all your preparation, prayer, research, and expertise are done, God will take over. He doesn't put words into your mouth unless you have done the hard work of Scripture memorization and investigation into the details of your subject matter. Once when I was teaching a weekly Bible class, I was amazed at the words that came out of my mouth. I had been privately memorizing a large section of Scripture, the first nine chapters of the book of Acts. The memorization attempt was a personal discipline that I wanted to do privately, and I told very few people about my memory project. As I was teaching my class, I suddenly quoted a few verses from Acts chapter 3. I had no plans to use those verses as a reference for that day's lesson, but because I stored the words away in my mind, God called them up at just the right moment.

Luke 4 tells us that the Spirit led Jesus. I know I can find my anointing when I am led by the Spirit of God to do what God has asked me to do, even if I don't understand why. Even if it doesn't fit into my plans. Even if it doesn't make sense to me.

Sweet Spot

You can speak as if God's words are yours when you know your calling, prepare fully, and watch for the connection with your audience. Sometimes when a person approaches me at the end of a presentation, they ask how they can become a speaker too. My reply usually surprises them. I tell them that speaking is a craft that must be learned. I suggest they get training. I say the messages are crafted and planned and every gesture and voice and facial expression is planned and practiced. Your words are too important to leave to chance. Careless empty words are useless. Use your words well. Only then can the Holy Spirit do His work as you speak. Become a devoted, passionate follower of Christ; present messages that center around your life's theme, and give answers and hope to your audiences.

Practice

1. Can you identify your sweet spot or your anointing? When does it occur?

2. Write a few sentences to describe your mission as a speaker.

3. What is the one overall theme that flows through all your messages?

4. Who are you becoming and what daily steps are you taking to walk close to God?

Chapter 5
Examples, Illustrations, Stories

Never allow critical thinking to interfere with creative thinking.

--McNair Wilson

Stories are the main way you will engage your audience. But telling stories for entertainment only isn't valuable to your overall presentation, unless you are a comedian. Every story must have a point. Every story must make the point you are presenting.

Early one morning, my Great Pyrenees dog fell into the swimming pool, and I had to haul her out even though the steps were within inches of her feet. It turned into a great illustration for a presentation on how we often act contrasted with what we should do when we encounter trouble. But I don't tell the story just for the fun of it. I tell it only to make my point clearer.

Does It Make Your Point?

Does the story you are using make the point of your message? If not, file it away for another time. An editor once told me, "Karen, the only reason you have that story in that chapter is because you like the story!" The editor was right. I really did like that story, but I realized the story didn't reinforce or illustrate my point. If the story doesn't make the point, then leave it out.

The best stories or illustrations come from your life. These life stories teach truth. Be alert to everything around you; examples to get your point across are everywhere. During a hurricane, my family and I evacuated. Now, stories from those adventures are part of my presentations, and the particular hurricane story I use will always relate the message of that presentation. If I'm speaking on fear or facing storms, I use one hurricane story. If I'm speaking on personal perspective, another part of those hurricane stories will be more effective.

Jesus lived His examples. His life showed His teaching. He used every situation and every detail to teach His messages. He began with His baptism as He came from Galilee to the Jordan to be baptized by John. Throughout His life, Jesus' story examples often showed the crowds what they were supposed to do. He understood the power of a story well told.

As you read of the events in Jesus' life, you will find many examples where He presented the truth by using a story. At one time, a centurion came to see Jesus because he believed Jesus could save his child from a life-threatening illness. Jesus pointed to the man then told His disciples on the spot, "Here is an example of faith."

Every situation in your life can become an example. Even situations that occur in the middle of your speaking event can become an example. I was teaching a class about humility using Philippians, and one of my students began singing a line from a country western song, *It's hard to be humble when you're perfect in every way.*[ii] It was a funny yet effective teaching moment.

Can the Audience Relate?

Jesus used familiar things such as lilies, bread, grass, and birds to illustrate His points. He knew His cultural and physical surroundings and used them to explain His message. The story of the speck and the log in the eye was a good example in His day because people knew that the temple gate was called the eye of the needle. Jesus used everyday references to make His points, and you can too.

When you use an example that relates to the audience, it will be powerful, memorable, and meaningful. It will reaffirm the point you are trying to make. When you go into a city to speak, do some research and understand the locale. Know about the local baseball team or that the city's basketball team is in the playoffs. Your audience will love you for knowing their world.

When talking to Simon Peter, a fisherman by trade, Jesus told Peter to take the boat out into the deep and put out the net. Jesus wanted to show Peter how to be a fisher of men. By using Peter's occupation and the terminology he would know, Jesus gave Peter a visual challenge to which he could relate.

When Peter saw the miracle of many fish, he was astounded and ready to hear what Jesus had to say.

> When they had done so, they caught such a large number of fish that their nets began to break. So they signaled their partners in the other boat to come and help them, and they came and filled both boats so full that they began to sink. When Simon Peter saw this, he fell at Jesus' knees and said, "Go away from me, Lord; I am a sinful man!" For he and all his companions were astonished at the catch of fish they had taken, and so were James and John, the sons of Zebedee, Simon's partners. Then Jesus said to Simon, "Don't be afraid; from now on you will fish for people." So they pulled their boats up on shore, left everything and followed him (Luke 5:6-11 NIV).

Jesus said, "From now on you will fish for people." Peter and his brother and other fishermen got the message and they followed Jesus. They believed His message. They understood the message's content because of the illustration. As a result, they became world-changers.

As you decide what illustrations to use, keep your audience in mind. Use what is familiar to *them* to make your points. Think about the types of things they likely will know, and not know. Remember the infamous faux pas by a national politician who told midwestern farmers to grow Belgian Endive instead of corn. Never mind that they could have grown enough endive to supply the whole country in just a few of their fields. He didn't understand his audience or their needs.

Did You Archive the Story?

Once you become aware of story examples, then record those examples or stories so you can retrieve them for later. Don't rely on your memory, no matter how good it is. In chapter one, I told the story of being in a hospital waiting room. I remember that story because as I sat in that drab gray room and observed all those people, I wrote down some notes. Later, I built my story about waiting around that scene.

If you are at a public event, notice the crowd around you. What are people doing? One time I was at a football game and saw a man who was apparently so disgusted with the team and the coach that every play he raised his hands and flipped his palms outward, saying, "Whatever!" It was so comical to watch. No matter what play the coach called or how the team executed it, the man was never impressed. He just shrugged them off, saying, "Whatever." I wrote this little story in my notebook. While I haven't figured out how to use it yet, except right here, I am sure the story will be a perfect illustration someday.

You can find stories in everything that happens to you. My friend Ken Davis was on a plane ready for takeoff when the flight was delayed because the airport crews needed to clean bugs off the wings. He found the humor in the details and then turned the story into a message about clearing the bugs out of our life. Read his blog post about it here.

If he can build an entertaining yet powerful message from bugs on a plane, you can find examples in your life too.

Keep a small notebook in your pocket or purse, so you can record the funny and interesting things you see. Also, keep a pad of paper and pen by your bedside for those thoughts that flash through your mind during the night. I know it's not fun to turn on the light or get your glasses so you can write down your thoughts, but if you don't, you will be even more annoyed when morning comes and you remember you got a wonderful idea during the night but can't remember what it is. You will never remember all the great things you observe during the day or the good ideas you get during the night unless you write them down.

If I get a good thought during the night or while I'm driving, I usually write down only a few words to describe the event. I write just enough so I'll remember the story. When morning comes or I arrive at my destination, then I take a few more moments to make sure I've recorded the essence of the story. When I get ready to use that story in a presentation, I will flesh out the details from my memory.

Is It Current?

What is your audience thinking about today? What do they want to know about now? One of the ways to see what people are talking about on any given day is to use Google Trends. Visit www.google.com/trends. This site lets you see the top searches that have been done that day on Google. The site is updated several times a day, and from it you can learn the questions the world is asking in real time. If it is a big sports day, such as the Super Bowl or NBA signing day, then the hot topics will be primarily about sports. If a famous person has made the news that day, then the searches will reflect it. Stay up to date, and watch these trends so you can pick and choose what is important to your presentations. You will have fresh, current, viable fodder to which you can refer.

Numerous websites are available to help you stay up to date. Check out www.trendhunter.com to see what's hot for the next holiday, products inspired by the latest movies, what collectors are searching for, and the latest in accessories. On Twitter, search the hashtag #trends to find the latest hot topic. Go to www.cnn.com/trends and www.indeed.com/jobtrends to find the latest news and job information. For information on fashion trends, go to www.style.com/trendsshopping. With access to the Internet, we, as speakers, have so much information available to help us make our presentations interesting and current.

Did You Evaluate Your Personal Life?

Your personal life makes the best illustrations because you know yourself intimately. Consider your past, and you will discover so many great examples. By answering the following questions, you can discover how your own life is a treasure chest of examples.

Where were you born?

How many siblings are in your family?

Where did you grow up (city, country, apartment complex, arm, etc.)?

What decade were you born in, and what was happening in the world at that time?

Describe your school.

Describe your friends.

What did you do for fun?

What was expected of you as a child – by your parents, teachers, and other adults in your life?

What factors contributed to the happiness or sadness of your childhood? Consider weight, financial situation, neighborhood, friends or lack of friends, or family dynamics.

How did you cope with unpleasant situations as a child? As a teen?

List some of your favorite activities as a child and as a teen.

Do you have expertise in any of the following areas?
Music

Health

Family relationships

Job hunting

Writing

Poetry

Sports

Outdoor activities

Dance

Your past is like a notebook full of illustrations from your personal story. Your present is a window, revealing examples and anecdotes. Your future is a doorway to rich stories that will enhance and illustrate future presentations.

Is the Story Well-Crafted?

According to Matthew 13:24, Jesus spoke in parables to reach the world. He was a storyteller. Are you a storyteller? Can you make your point with a well-crafted story? Once you've decided to use a story as an illustration or example, it will need some work to put it in a good format.

When you craft a story, figure out how to twist the story so your hearers can't anticipate your ending. Jesus told the people to give to the needy in secret and not let anyone see them do it because God would see instead. His emphasis on giving in secret was a twist they didn't expect. And the person who listened and practiced what He taught would be forever changed.

How can you change your story's ending to make your audience take notice? Can you add a surprise? Can you twist the words or the meanings? What if you changed it completely?

Telling a good story as an illustration requires crafting the story. It should have characters, scenes, a sequence of happenings, progress, emotional conflict, and a point (and a surprising twist, if possible). Start each story with a description of normal. Then add an element of conflict. Then resolve the conflict and bring the story to a new normal.

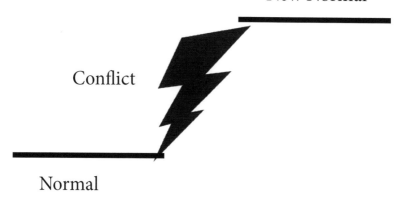

New Normal

Conflict

Normal

Notice the details of one of Jesus' parables.

> Or suppose a woman has ten silver coins
> and loses one. Won't she light a lamp and
> sweep the entire house and search carefully
> until she finds it? And when she finds it, she
> will call in her friends and neighbors and
> say, "Rejoice with me because I have found
> my lost coin." In the same way, there is joy
> in the presence of God's angels when even
> one sinner repents (Luke 15:8-10 NLT).

Characters:	A woman, her neighbors
Scene:	The woman's house
Sequence of Events:	Loses a coin, finds the coin, rejoices with neighbors
Point:	There is joy in the presence of God's angels when one sinner repents

Notice how the story is put together. First, we get the description of normal life. A woman in a household possesses some coins. Then comes the conflict. She loses one of the coins. She lights a lamp and sweeps the house, searching until she finds the coin. When she finds it, the story reaches a new normal. She celebrates with her neighbors because the coin has been found. The point is clear and spiritually deep.

Every story must have these elements. Without understanding what the normal was, we can't understand the trauma of the conflict. And without conflict, a story is boring. After the conflict, all stories must resolve in some way.

When crafting your story, add a beginning and an ending and some dramatic elements, such as sound effects, accents, and soft or loud voice inflections.

Let's craft a story about my Great Pyrenees falling into the pool:

> The morning is dusky and foggy as I let Isabelle out the back door. She typically comes back fast because she is afraid of noises and the dark and especially of water. When I open the door again, she doesn't come. Then I see her in the swimming pool.
>
> Somehow she has fallen in and now she is clinging to the side of the pool, her paws digging into the concrete. I run to her because I know she is terrified of water. I notice that her back feet are one inch from some steps and I try to get her to swing one foot over just a bit so she can push herself out of the pool. She won't budge. I consider prying her front paws from the edge of the pool because I know she can swim and could easily paddle to the other steps nearby. Instead, I take pity on her and reach down and lift her out of the pool.

Using these basic story facts, I can craft a story that will illustrate my message.

The Beginning

How can I grab my audience's attention? I begin the story by announcing in a loud voice, "Isabelle is a wuss!"

Normal

I describe how she hides in the closet when it thunders and is frightened by a loud noise or how she runs for cover when a loud truck drives by. I never describe Isabelle, but I speak of her in human terms, so it is a while before the audience realizes that Isabelle is a dog. Some people don't realize it until I show her photo on the screen.

Conflict

I weave the story around the early morning scene using descriptions of the fog and semi-darkness and how Isabelle looked hanging on the side of the pool – claws trying to dig into the concrete side of the pool.

Points

I make three points about the incident.

First point: If Isabelle would have moved one of her back legs just an inch or so, she would have been able to get the footing necessary to push herself out of the pool. Application: The answer to our troubled situation is often nearby too. If we will just look around us, we might find the answer and raise ourselves out of our trouble.

Second point: Isabelle knows how to swim. We taught her and worked with her long enough so she could always turn around to find the big steps. Application: Sometimes when we are in trouble, we can solve the problem by drawing on the skills, expertise, and talents within us. All we need to do is calm down and move in the direction of our training to get to safety.

Third point: On that morning I had mercy on Isabelle and reached down, placing my strong arms beneath her and lifting her out. Application: Sometimes when we are in trouble, God has mercy on us as frail human beings. "He reached down from on high and took hold of me; he drew me out of deep waters" (Psalm 18:16 NIV).

54

Ending

When trouble strikes, look around to find a way to push yourself out or swim to safety using the skills you have already acquired. Or cry out to God for mercy and He will rescue you. But don't be a wuss!

Did you notice how the conflict interrupted the normal and a line in the ending reminds the hearers of the opening? To hear an audio version of this story go to http://speaklikeJesus.com

Did You Prune Extra Details from the Story?

Jesus used examples on the spot, but He was careful not to allow those listening to get sidetracked by extra details. One day He was in the temple, watching people as they walked to the offering plate or box. It was the norm in that time for religious people to make a big show of their offering by dropping coins loudly and lingering long, so everyone would see them. Jesus took that moment to teach about what pleases God. He said, "When you give to the needy, don't let anyone see you. God will see" (my paraphrase). The twist on the normal procedure made the truth much stronger. If a person followed Jesus' practical application, his or her life would be changed.

Notice that Jesus did *not* mention what people were wearing or what the people may or may not have been saying. Jesus drew attention *only* to the details that were necessary for His point, which was humility.

Be able to tell your story long and short so you can use it in different situations. When I tell the audience about my corporate job coming to an end after a foreign company purchased the company where I'd worked for more than 30 years, I carefully crafted the full story so that I could tell it in about six minutes. Once I was asked to speak for five minutes total. I wanted to tell this story, so I cut out every extraneous detail and was able to tell the story in two and one-half minutes. Combined with my outline, this story became part of my five-minute talk.

The Apostle Paul told his conversion story many times in the New Testament. He told it in great detail on some occassions, but he could also tell it in a few words, (see 1 Timothy 1:12-14). His outline was always the same: What I was; what happened to me; what I am now.

Commercials on TV often tell a story. The producers will prepare a 90-second version, which is the full story, and after it has aired for a while, they will also air the 60-second and 30-second versions. The story is the same but in an abbreviated form. Sometimes we don't have time for all the details.

As you prepare your stories and illustrations, ask yourself, "Can I tell it short?"

What Makes a Good Story?

First and foremost, a good story must make a point. Never tell a story just because it is funny or cute or because you like it. Does it make the point of your message? If not, file it away for another time. Use a personal story or illustration from your own experience only when you know that your story will lead the audience to their own story. The bridge between your story and theirs is critical to the success of your illustration.

You can find examples in the situations and scenery around you and in the people you meet and observe. Everything that happens to you is a potential story, especially if you notice the funny and dramatic things around you. Stories are everywhere.

Become a Great Storyteller

Stories are important because they make hearers apply the deeper message of the presentation. Story is the chief way you can capture the heart of your audience. Story makes the point stick and the action become achievable.

Our brains are wired to hear and respond to story – not bullet points. In fact, it is rare for a hearer to remember the points of a presentation, but the same person will store away all the truth in a story and will make a personal connection between the story and his or her own life situation.

Stories are better than facts, or statistics, or logic, or even sales pitches. Think about the commercials that you remember above all the others. They almost always have a story woven in. Top marketers know that they must tell a story if they are going to have successful sales. They know this because they know that people react and respond to story. You need to understand this principle and use story as much as possible in your presentation.

Jesus understood clearly that story was the key to good communication. He used parables throughout His ministry, and He never lectured. Mark 4:34 says storytelling was His primary method. His messages were rich with theology and instruction, but story made the message clear and applicable.

Think about some of His familiar stories. The Good Samaritan for example. When we hear that story, we understand the clear teaching of love and compassion and the wrongness of passing on the other side when someone is in trouble.

When we hear the story of the shepherd with a hundred sheep who loses one and goes after it even though he still has ninety-nine, we understand the loving care of our Great Shepherd.

When we see the foolishness of the builder who built his house in the sand, we get it and apply the truth that we need a good foundation to survive the storms of life.

The prodigal son acts like many of us did when we were young, but when we see the young man's father running down the road to meet him, we are touched by the love of God who will never give up on us.

Stories should never be made up. Your audience will recognize fiction. Stories should never be a joke or copied from a book or read from the emails that fill your in-box or flood Facebook. These stories are often shallow and uninteresting and some in the audience will have read the story. Use your own stories. What happened to you? An amazing true story will make your point and change lives.

Your life is full of illustrations. Something is always happening around you. Open your eyes to see it. Children, family, books, sports, history, the news, movies, radio, television—all these are places to find stories that apply to your message.

Illustrate with Stories

Well-crafted stories are crucial to the success of your presentations. When deciding which story to use, ask if it makes your point and whether the audience can relate. Then, using the elements of story, craft a strong, interesting story with characters, scene, and a poignant point. Eliminate every extraneous detail from the story. Look for stories everywhere (including your life, past and present) and record them in a notebook. Work on your storytelling skills.

Practice

1. Think back over the past 48 hours. What happened that could be used as an illustration in your next talk? Craft a two-minute illustration, using the three elements of story.

2. Buy a small notebook in which you can record stories and events. Put a pen and pad on the table near your bed.

3. Review a story you've told in a presentation. Does it have the elements of story: normal/conflict/new normal? Did you use characters, scene, and the five senses to tell the story? What can you prune out of the story to make it shorter?

4. Time one of your stories or illustrations as you tell it out loud. Now tell the same story but use one full minute longer to tell it by inserting pauses.

Chapter 6
Powerful, Poetic Words

**The limits of my language mean the
limits of my world.**

-- Ludwig Wittgenstein

Presentations are made of words, so the words you use are important. Find a fresh, powerful way to present your message by using creative analogies, quotations from others, lyrical terms, repetition, powerful verbs, and other techniques. When you use new words to say things in unusual ways, then your audience has the opportunity to experience that truth anew.

Words have Power

Emily Dickinson said, "I know nothing in the world that has as much power as a word." She was right. A word fitly spoken is capable of building a person up and inspiring them to new endeavors. It is important for us to use precise language – not a word that's kinda what we mean. We get lazy and fall back on our limited language when using a thesaurus would help us find the perfect word to convey our meaning. We sometimes settle for the most common, boring words.

Become a student of language. When you hear someone speak, consider the words they used. Did they inspire or challenge you? Did they spur your curiosity? Read good literature and good writers. Consider reading or re-reading the classics to increase the scope of your vocabulary. Think of every word you plan to say in your presentation. Is there a stronger verb or a more descriptive noun that would say it better?

But, you might say, there is nothing new under the sun. How then can you revive and reinvigorate your content?

Analogies

An analogy means a comparison or similarity between two dissimilar things. One way to give your content a *makeover* is to use an overarching analogy to *brush* your presentation with *color* by comparing each *feature* or point of your presentation to an item familiar to your audience. (I used a makeup metaphor in the previous sentence by choosing verbs and nouns to relate speaking to cosmetics. A metaphor is like an analogy but on a smaller scale.) But a cosmetics analogy isn't a good choice for an audience of men. So you might choose a rock-climbing analogy. In each of your points, choose nouns and verbs that relate your content to elements of rock-climbing.

Whatever analogy you make, be sure to keep it consistent throughout your presentation. Don't make a rock-climbing analogy for your first point, then a gardening analogy, and then a sewing analogy. If you mix your analogies, then your audience will get confused and your presentation will seem unfocused.

Quotations

When using a quotation from someone that gives your topic power and reference, use it well. First, learn it well so that you can quote it in a dramatic or powerful voice. Second, don't use the entire quote if part of it doesn't apply. If one phrase or part of the quote makes your point, don't distract from it by giving the part of the quote that doesn't fit. Practice speaking the quote aloud so you can present it with power and clarity. Practice using pauses in various places in the quote. Practice emphasizing different words. Be sure you can pronounce every word clearly.

Earlier in this chapter, I quoted Emily Dickinson. The quote I used was only part of a longer quote.

> I know nothing in the world that has as
> much power as a word. Sometimes I write
> one, and I look at it, until it begins to
> shine.

Because we are talking about speaking, I didn't use the second part of the quote. Dickinson was a great writer, and her focus was on writing, but her statement about the power of a word is appropriate in our context. There was no need for me to muddy the waters by using the rest of the quote.

Read this quote from Tom Stoppard's *The Real Thing: A Play*.

> Words…they're innocent, neutral, precise, standing for this, describing that, meaning the other, so if you look after them you can build bridges across incomprehension and chaos. But when they get their corners knocked off, they're no good any more…I don't think writers are sacred, but words are. They deserve respect. If you get the right ones in the right order, you can nudge the world a little or make a poem, which children will speak for you when you're dead.

The quote is an example of a quote that I could use as an example in this chapter. It speaks of the power of words and how getting the right ones in the right order could change the world. I love the quote but I won't use it in a speech. It is too long. It brings in concepts that might get my audience off track such as *words being sacred; words needing respect;* and *poems, which children will quote.* You will lose the attention of your audience if you use a quote that is too long and too complex. Pare it down or don't use it.

Don't give long explanations or dwell on the name of the person you are quoting unless there is a story associated with the quote that fits your point.

Verbal Images

Jesus used verbal images throughout His ministry. He described events, situations, persons, and places with language that took the

61

audience there with Him. Notice His picturesque language in the following verses:

> When you pray, don't be like the hypocrites who love to pray publicly on street corners and in the synagogues where everyone can see them. I tell you the truth; that is all the reward they will ever get. But when you pray, go away by yourself, shut the door behind you, and pray to your Father in private. Then your Father, who sees everything, will reward you (Matthew 6:5-6 NLT).

Notice the description. You can see the street corners in your mind and the proud hypocrite making a spectacle. You also visualize the humble person in the private room with the door closed and you can imagine God smiling as He looks on. Jesus' words paint a picture for your mind—a verbal visual.

Jesus' description of the light and darkness in the passage below helps us understand the desperation of following the wrong path:

> Your eye is a lamp that provides light for your body. When your eye is good, your whole body is filled with light. But when your eye is bad, your whole body is filled with darkness. And if the light you think you have is actually darkness, how deep that darkness is! (Matthew 6:22-23 NLT).

The sensory details in these verses paint a picture like an artist paints a portrait. The eye is a lamp and when you see beautiful, good, noble things, it lights up the entire body. But if you look with lust, hate, unforgiveness, your entire being is filled with darkness. And we are easily fooled about whether something is light or dark. Jesus' poetic descriptive words are better than a media presentation. His words transport us to the scene He paints.

Poetic Language

Jesus used poetic language, imagery, illustration, and lyrical words to give His messages. Read these words from the Sermon on the Mount aloud to get a feel for the poetry and rhythm.

> Blessed are the poor in spirit, for theirs is the kingdom of heaven.
>
> Blessed are those who mourn, for they will be comforted.
>
> Blessed are the meek, for they will inherit the earth.
>
> Blessed are those who hunger and thirst for righteousness, for they will be filled.
>
> Blessed are the merciful, for they will be shown mercy.
>
> Blessed are the pure in heart, for they will see God.
>
> Blessed are the peacemakers, for they will be called children of God.
>
> Blessed are those who are persecuted because of righteousness, for theirs is the kingdom of heaven.
>
> Blessed are you when people insult you, persecute you and falsely say all kinds of evil against you because of me.
>
> Rejoice and be glad, because great is your reward in heaven, for in the same way they persecuted the prophets who were before you (Matthew 5:2-11 NIV).

Notice the rhythm of using the same sentence structure and the same word to begin each point: "Blessed are…." See the contrasts in the words He used: mourn-comforted; hungry-filled; mercy given-mercy received. Observe the twists and surprises: poor in spirit will be heirs of the kingdom; pure in heart will see God; peacemakers will be called children of God.

The rhythm, repetition, flow, poetry, musical quality, and cadence are all part of these timeless words. These words are often and easily memorized. They are simple yet deeply profound.

Twists or Contrasts

Jesus used twists and contrasting terms. Twists make the truth stronger. Twists can also provide an element of surprise. Here is a surprising twist. We don't expect it, so this statement makes us pause to think.

Notice the twists and contrasts in The Beatitudes.

Blessed are the poor in spirit – for theirs is the kingdom of heaven.

The contrast—the twist—is between the poor and kingdom owners. The hope those words inspire is huge. A few verses down we find a contrast between mourning and comfort. Jesus offered an answer to grief. Grief will end in comfort. Pain is replaced by peace. Again, this contrast gives hope, a reason to keep going. Jesus said those who are meek will inherit the earth. That means they will have great power. See the contrast? Normally, we think those who are meek appear weak (although the true definition of meekness is strength under control).

In another place, Jesus compared wrong and right prayer. Don't stand like the hypocrites who stand to be seen; instead, go into a closet and pray in private. He told what not to do: Don't use empty phrases. Then He told what to do: the model prayer.

Gracious words came from His mouth. So much so that people were amazed. "Is this Joseph's son?" They were amazed at His ability. God will give you the ability you need too. Our son, Brett, is a pastor and church planter in Canada. We are amazed every time we hear him preach. God has given him ability beyond what we knew.

Good Orators

Occasionally, on the political scene in America, a figure will emerge who has exceptional oratory skills. Using the QR code here, go to the videos showing some well-known American politicians who had good oratory skills.

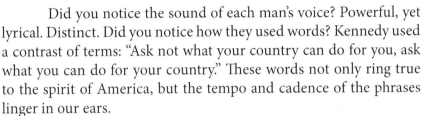

Did you notice the sound of each man's voice? Powerful, yet lyrical. Distinct. Did you notice how they used words? Kennedy used a contrast of terms: "Ask not what your country can do for you, ask what you can do for your country." These words not only ring true to the spirit of America, but the tempo and cadence of the phrases linger in our ears.

Ronald Reagan was a master communicator who used his skills as a trained actor to modulate his voice. He knew when to speak loudly, when to soften the phrase, and when to pause. His challenge to Mr. Gorbachov about the Berlin wall echoes through the years: "Tear down this wall!" Such a short sentence and simple words yet it is filled with power and strength. Reagan mastered storytelling. It is said that his speechwriters would write the major policy points he needed to make and then write, "Tell a story here," in his speech manuscripts. He was so adept at telling a story that made the point that they didn't have to prepare it for him. Your audiences are accustomed to stories from books, magazines, TV, radio, and movies. They love to relate a principle to a story.

Marco Rubio is a young politician who has learned many of the skills needed to capture the attention of an audience. Did you feel the rhythm? His mannerisms and sentence structures are almost musical. If you didn't catch it, go back and listen to him again with an eye and ear for the rhythm and tempo of his voice.

Words, Words

As you construct your presentations, consider ways you can use the techniques Jesus used to make your language more lyrical or poetic by using analogies, repetition, contrasts, twists, surprises, and powerful language. These language tricks make the truth more relevant, more understandable, and more memorable.

Practice

1. Go to the website http//speaklikeJesus.com. Read through the lists of powerful verbs and persuasive nouns. Which ones could you incorporate into your next presentation?

2. Review one of your recent presentations. What quotes did you use? Should they be shortened to make them more pointed and powerful?

3. Choose a subject from the list below and write a sentence using powerful verbs and strong nouns. Write the sentence as if someone might quote you on the subject.

> Fear
>
> Fortune
>
> Power
>
> Healthy Living
>
> Faith
>
> Bitterness
>
> Forgiveness
>
> Purity

Chapter 7
Stage Presence

***He had this kind of stage presence
where you couldn't ignore it.
He walked onstage, he looked
dangerous. You just didn't know
what he was going to do.***

--Neil Innes

One day Jesus was preaching along the shore. More people joined the throngs who pressed in. When the crowd got too large, Jesus got into a boat and pushed out into the edges of the water. He used that boat as a stage or pulpit. Then the entire crowd could see and hear His message. He utilized the speaking platform He had to its best advantage.

Arrive Early

You need to be aware and comfortable with the stage setting for your presentation. Arrive early at the venue where you will speak so you can check out the stage, the microphones, the podium, the lighting, and the general space.

The first rule of stage preparation is for you *not* to be a prima dona. Do not demand or make ultimatums for things that will cause your hosts to wish they'd never invited you. Instead, make the best of whatever situation you find yourself in by thinking carefully before you spout off the first need that comes into your mind. Seek to make the best possible scenario for that event. Ask nicely for changes in the stage arrangement or for the lighting or the microphone to be changed, but never be demanding or severe.

I spoke at a community organization fund raiser. Before the event, I made my way to the stage and discovered a runway for a fashion show that would be presented prior to my presentation. The podium set up for me to speak from was wedged between two walls of flowers and stuck at the back of the stage, so there would be plenty of room for the runway. If I stood behind that podium, I knew I would never make any eye contact with the large crowd nor would half of them even be able to see me wedged in between the bouquets of flowers. My only choice was to stand at the end of the runway, and the evening was a great success because I connected with the audience.

Since I was speaking to a nonprofit group, I knew the event budget was limited. I knew I needed to make the best of the situation I had been given. I laid my IPad down and walked to the end of the runway and presented my talk without using the notes. I knew my outline. I knew my illustrations and references, so I gave my talk without the aid of notes. You will be able to do this kind of spur-of-the-moment change if you know your material well and if you have a dynamite outline that allows you to remember what you want to say next, and if you have your opening and closing memorized.

Check the Lighting and Podium

Before the event, as you stand on the stage, look at the lights. The best lighting is at 45-degree angles. If the lighting leaves you in a dark spot, talk to the technician and see if you can get it changed. If not, move to a different place on the stage to get better lighting that doesn't cause shadows.

If at all possible, remove the podium from the stage. If others are going to use the podium or you feel you must have some notes, try to get a short table placed on the stage for you. If the podium is the only thing available, ask someone to move it to the side so there is no barrier between you and the audience. Never ever lean on a podium.

Look in the Mirror

Your clothing, hairstyle, and appearance need to be neat and stylish. Women, be sure your makeup is appropriate for the situation. You may need a bit more than usual if the lights are strong. Men, make sure your tie is straight and check those zippers one more time.

Ask your assistant or a trusted friend to give you one last "look-over" before you go on stage. If everything is buttoned, zipped, and in place, walk on stage with confidence.

Move with Purpose

Use the stage as part of your message. Every inch of the platform is an empty canvas waiting for you to paint the picture for your audience. Movement is a sign of life. Moving on a stage is important, but pacing back and forth or rocking is distracting. Move with purpose. Walk to one side of the stage and look at the crowd. Finish the thought or sentence before you turn to move again. After the thought is finished, walk to the middle or the other side of the stage. Always look in the direction you are going. Never walk one direction and look the other direction.

Use a Neutral Position

While movement is good, it is also important to find a neutral place on the stage and stay there. This spot should be where you start and where you return when you move. This spot is neutral. Go there often.

In addition, find a comfortable body position that will become your neutral position. Take that stance often, too. It may be hands at your side or in some other comfortable natural position. When you make a hand gesture to emphasize a point, return to neutral as soon as possible.

Be cautious of your movements in a room that is fan-shaped. If the stage is circular and there are people on both sides to the extreme left and right, you will have a tendency to pace back and forth because of the wide area of the crowd. Force yourself to stand still and move to each side with purpose.

I understand this principle of stage presence and have practiced it over and over to get the perfect balance between movement and standing still. Yet I recently spoke in a church auditorium, which had an audience seating arrangement of about 180 degrees. Even though I knew better, the video of that event shows me pacing back and forth nervously trying to include every audience member every time. The result was frenetic pacing. Make a conscious effort to limit your pacing and movements.

Concentrate on standing still. Nervous pacing even one step each way or rocking back and forth worries and distracts your audience.

Check the Floor

Be aware of the stage. What else is on stage with you? Musical instruments, podiums, decorations, wires, speakers, and such can trip you up if you haven't carefully evaluated the space you have to move around. Be particularly observant about holes in the stage floor. Perhaps there are sections to the stage, which leave gaps when put together. Or maybe there are indentions for wiring and other technical things. Carefully walk over the area before your presentation, and make sure your heel will not sink or get stuck in any crevices or gaps.

Make the best of any situation without being petty or demanding. I'm sure standing in a boat on the water wasn't ideal for Jesus, but He made the best choice for His situation, much better than being pushed out to sea by a crowd.

Finish on Time

You must finish on time. Use a phone, watch, or countdown clock. Even if you start late, finish on time. The event planner will love you for it. If you organize your presentation well using the techniques in this book, you can give your message in ten minutes or thirty minutes because you only expand or shrink the message by the number of examples you give or stories you tell.

Practice

1. Watch yourself on video. Do you notice any recurring hand or body movements? Ask a friend if these movements are annoying. Watching the video in fast-forward will help catch those moves that might irritate your audience.

2. Take acting classes or get a coach to help you make fluid, meaningful movements on the stage.

3. Practice one of your favorite stories and use exaggerated hand and body movements. Then choose one or two that work and adjust them to use next time you tell the story on stage. Keep one or two that work.

Chapter 8
Technology

Beauty of style and harmony and grace and good rhythm depend on simplicity.

--Plato

Jesus' baptism was the biggest multimedia event in history. The heavens split apart and the voice of God said, "This is my beloved son in whom I am well pleased." Then the Spirit descended on Him like a dove. (See Matthew 1:10-13.)

What a dramatic, big, spectacular event. No one would ever forget. You can't re-produce this event, but you can use sight, sounds, and signs. You can be dramatic and big and spectacular. You can use words, stories, props, actions, or media to help the audience remember your point long after they've left the auditorium.

Media enhances presentations. Use all of it you can—video, audio, Power Point (Keynote), props, and visual aids. Your audience is accustomed to media through TV, movies, the Internet, and in church. If you present with a lecture only, then you have missed an opportunity to connect visually and give auditory stimulation to your audience.

Learn to use today's technology. Be familiar enough so you can troubleshoot problems. But be prepared enough so that if your planned technology doesn't work, then you can give your presentation without the media dazzle. Don't rely on the media. If it goes wrong, do your presentation anyway.

The Peril and Power of Power Point

I once saw a well-known national speaker stand mutely on the stage for nearly 15 minutes while technicians struggled with making the projector work. By the time they got it working, she had lost her audience and never regained it. Media is used to enhance and illustrate and make your presentation more exciting, but media is *not* your presentation. Power Point (or Keynote), especially, is not your presentation.

Power Point (or Keynote) is a wonderful tool, but it has been misused in boardrooms and meeting rooms from its beginning. Attend any corporate business meeting and you will see what I mean. Often tiny print or intricate spreadsheets are squeezed onto the screen and no one can see them or read the tiny print or understand what the point is. And then in many business presentations, the speaker simply reads the Power Point screen. How boring!

Learn to use Power Point well. I recommend a book by Garth Reynolds titled *Presentation Zen* to help you understand the strength of Power Point and to help you understand how misusing it can kill your presentation. All media should enhance the presentation. This means you must use photographs and graphic visuals to make the point without using many words on a screen. Your audience cannot listen to what you say, take notes, and read a screen full of written words all at the same time. Instead of using a screen full of words (or even bullet points), present a photo that depicts the message without any words on the screen. If you must use words, keep them to a minimum of two to four on each screen.

For example, in one presentation I stress that God never gives us a look at the whole future He has planned for us, but He expects us to take one step at a time. I show a full-screen photo of a forest. The underbrush, vines, and plants are so thick you could not move forward if you were there. This scene depicts how our next step looks to us: We cannot see the future. God never asks us to see the whole future; He only asks that we exert enough faith to take one step into the dense darkness. As we do, He opens up a path. In fact, if we take the steps one at a time in faith, He will make our path smooth. (See Psalm 119:105.) I always tell my audience that after we have taken those steps into the unknown future, we can turn around and see how God has opened the way. Then I show a photo of a lighted highway. The contrast between the two photos is a dramatic way for each person to see what God does when we step out in faith. The two photos emphasize your speech and handout – no words on the screen needed.

Power Point Structure:

> Pictures not words
>
> Few bullet points
>
> Big visual images

When building a Power Point (or Keynote), use the rule of thirds. Artists and photographers divide images into thirds both vertically and horizontally with lines that look like a tic-tack-toe board. Your main images should appear along these lines and at the intersections of the lines. (These intersection points are called, strangely enough, power points.)

POWERPOINT

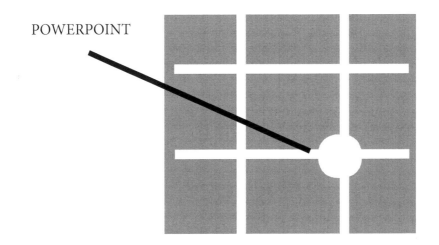

Rule of Thirds

Not only is the rule of thirds more pleasing to the eye, but it gives you room to place labels or other graphics.

The Vivid Visuals of Video

Adding some well-placed video clips in your presentation adds energy. To do this, learn your equipment, learn the software, and check with your host to be sure the facility is equipped for media.

It is important to embed videos into your presentation rather than relying on the Wi-Fi or Internet connections. The technology to embed videos isn't difficult. Learn it.

One of the most engaging church messages I ever heard was a sermon that compared a movie about a solo rock climber who got his hand wedged between two boulders to our life's choices. The presenter described portions of the story and then showed a short movie clip that captured just the point he wanted to make. He repeated the pattern about three times during his twenty- to thirty-minute presentation. Each clip was precisely chosen and edited. Before each clip, he prepared the audience by setting the scene without getting bogged down in details that didn't relate. After each clip, he made the analogy to our spiritual journeys and choices. The vivid, well-used video made it such a powerful presentation. And if the power had gone out in the room or if there had been some other technical glitch, I'm certain the speaker would have just kept going and told the story using descriptive language.

The Awesome Audio Clip

When used well, audio clips will capture an audience in a way nothing else can. Consider a well-placed sound effect or dramatic music from a movie or symphony or a line or two from a song to enhance your point. Using audio of someone speaking is tricky. Be careful not to use too long a segment if all you have is voice.

Combining Media

Singer and actress Bonnie Keen uses a combination of video and live audio well in a presentation where her alter-ego (an on-screen Bonnie) argues with the in-person Bonnie on the stage. The effect is funny yet powerful.

What creative way could you use media in your next presentation?

Master Multi-media

Take a class or go through tutorials on the Internet to learn as much as you can about the visual media you will be using. Learn how to use audio and video as well as Power Point. The more you know, the less likely you will be to encounter problems. The more you understand, the better you can use the technology.

Practice

1. Pick out a scene from a favorite movie and consider how you could use it as a video component in your next presentation.

2. Search your local community college or continuing education class catalogue to find a beginners media course you can take.

3. Go online and search for step-by-step instructions on how to embed video into a Power Point presentation. Practice this skill until you have it mastered.

Chapter 9
Openings

The last thing one discovers in composing a work is what to put first.

--Blaise Pascal, *Pens`ees*

The opening words you utter when you take the stage are critical to whether or not an audience will listen to you. You have only a few seconds to grab their attention. Within those few seconds, they will decide if they like you and whether or not they think you have something to say. Never use those precious few seconds in a frivolous way.

If you use the opening to apologize ("I'm not really a speaker…"), then you will never gain the trust of the audience. If you talk about the weather ("Isn't this cold in May crazy!"), then you will be perceived as bland. If you begin by thanking the event planner and team and commenting on the decorations ("Isn't it fun to see all the different tables?"), the audience will assume you are going to bore them with the obvious throughout the presentation.

Don't start with a lot of chitchat. Instead, engage your audience immediately. Don't waste the precious moments of your opening. No apologies, no flattery, no stalling. Begin immediately with a powerful, brief, clear, interesting opening to capture the audience's attention.

Use a Dynamic Opening

Jesus used great openings. When He wanted to comment on the shallowness of the religious rules set up by the rabbis, He didn't begin by saying, "You know all these rules that the rabbis have set up? I'm here to tell you there is more to living righteously than rules."

Instead, He opened with intriguing words.

> **You have heard that it was said,** 'Love your neighbor and hate your enemy.' **But I tell you,** love your enemies and pray for those who persecute you (Matthew 5:43 NIV, emphasis mine).

A great opening is like a fuse that gets your audience fired up. The opening is the only chance you have to make your audience want to hear your presentation. Make it memorable! The difference between a great opening and a lifeless one is the difference between the excitement of saying, "Once upon a time…" and the boredom of, "Now open your book to page ten just like we did last week." Your audience will either sit on the edge of their seats, excited to hear what you have to say, or they will settle back and expect more of the "same old-same old" they've always heard.

Establish Need

Why are you there to speak? Why should the audience listen? Is there a problem they want an answer for? Is there a solution you have discovered? Are you an expert that has information they want?

Show the audience how you will help them through whatever problem you introduced in your opening. Imagine if you had begun your presentation by saying, "A tornado has been spotted in our area!" You would have the audience's attention and they would be concerned, frightened, and ready to panic. They would be looking to you for direction. But you don't want to leave them hanging. Immediately, you would want to say, "I'll show you four ways to find a safe place."

A powerful opening line will startle listeners. They will pay attention. And then you can quickly move on by telling them how you will help them, how you will meet their need. There are many ways to start a presentation. Some good methods include using statistics, shocking statements, questions, stories, or quotations.

State Statistics

"One in three people will develop lung disease."

"More than half of the people in this room will face divorce or separation in marriage."

"Only 1 percent of teenage girls desire to become a homemaker."

Statistics are a great opening when you state them powerfully in a way that the audience instantly grabs the meaning. When using statistics, be intentional about how you present them. Instead of listing the statistics, interpret them. What does the statistic mean to the audience? Don't say them in confusing ways: "Out of 3,765 people surveyed, 1,028 answered. Of those 1,028 who responded, 924 said they…" Your audience will try to do the math and will miss whatever you say next. Instead of using numbers, make the point powerful by giving the analysis. "One-third of the population will…" If you can involve the audience, they will remember the statistic, "Look at your neighbor – one of you won't be back next year. Fifty percent of people don't renew membership."

If you can add humor to the statistic, it will become even more powerful. An older man gave the statistic that 79 percent of single adults live together before getting married. Then he said, "Back in my day, they called it 'shacking up!'" He countered the dismal statistic with the humor, but those of us who heard him speak never forgot the statistic.

Adding humor helps a statistic stick. Did you know the number one fear most people have is public speaking? In a survey, 41 percent of people named it as their number one fear. In that same survey, only 19 percent listed death as their number one fear. So Jerry Seinfeld said, "That means at a funeral, the person giving the eulogy would rather be in the casket!"

Use stats within a story. In a battle between story and stats, story would win every time.

Make a Shocking Statement

As soon as you reach the center of the stage, say something that surprises your audience. A pastor came to the stage, took a long look at the crowd, and shouted, "What in the world is wrong with you?" He paused to let the words sink in and then said, "Those are the words my wife said to me this week when I..." Then he built a message around the story.

Remember the story of my Great Pyrenees? The beginning sentence for this presentation is: "Isabelle is a wuss!" I proceed to tell how scared Isabelle is of loud noises and sudden movements. Later in the story, the audience learns that Isabelle is a dog. The story of her falling into the swimming pool is the basis for a three-point message on trusting God. My opening sentence works because my audience assumes Isabelle is a person and they are shocked that I would publicly label someone in such an unkind way.

Ask Questions

A question is a great tool for opening lines. It engages the audience and gets everyone focused on the subject matter.

> "How many of you are grandmothers? Who knew it would be such a great experience! It's your reward for not killing your children!"

When asking a question of your audience, raise your hand as if you were about to answer the question, and lean toward the audience. This will signal to them (1) that you are about to ask a question; and (2) that they should respond by raising their hands.

Use a Story

Beginning your presentation with a well-told story will engage and captivate your audience. Be sure that the story fits your message and that the point in the story is clearly part of your message. When you tell the story, use descriptive, colorful, emotional words.

When coaching a group about living excellently, I begin with this story:

> I once tried a new cheesecake recipe. The ingredients were expensive – several kinds of imported cheeses, special cream, and twelve eggs. I began mixing it all together and as I put in the last egg, I noticed that it didn't quite look right. Have you ever seen a "pretty good" egg? Something about the

color and the look of it seemed a little off. But then I thought about all the expensive ingredients that were already in the mixture and I really needed that cheesecake for a party, so I stirred the egg in. That night when the cheesecake was served, I couldn't eat any because I knew about the less-than-excellent egg.

After telling the story, I challenge my audience to reach for excellence (and I can't resist calling it "egg-cellence" at least once during the presentation), to always continue learning, and to never settle for second best. The opening story is the catalyst for the points.

Quote a Quotation

A quotation can be a powerful hook to grab your audience's attention, especially when you use your voice to add drama and pathos.

My friend Lael Arrington speaks about living large and squeezing all the best out of life. She often begins her presentation with a C. S. Lewis quote.

> We are half-hearted creatures, fooling about with drink and sex and ambition like an ignorant child who wants to go on making mud pies in a slum because he cannot imagine what is meant by the offer of a holiday at the sea.

Her audiences are intrigued by this powerful quote and the stunning way she quotes it.

******

Brainstorm how you might use one of the following quotes as a beginning to a presentation.

Be yourself; everyone else is already taken.–Oscar Wilde

A person may think their own ways are right, but the LORD weighs the heart (Proverbs 21:2).

A friend is someone who knows all about you and still loves you–Elbert Hubbard

A woman is like a tea bag; you never know how strong it is until its in hot water.–Eleanor Roosevelt

I have not failed. I've just found 10,000 ways that won't work.–Thomas A. Edison

If you judge people, you have no time to love them.–Mother Teresa

A bird doesn't sing because it has an answer, it sings because it has a song.–Maya Angelou

A fool finds pleasure in wicked schemes, but a person of understanding delights in wisdom (Proverbs 10:23).

Use Drama

A dramatic beginning will captivate your audience. Consider the difference between introducing your topic by saying, "I'm going to talk to you today about security in schools," or by saying,

> "Tobacco." (long pause)
>
> "Alcohol." (long pause)
>
> "Guns." (long pause)
>
> "These are the items seized in a sixth-grade locker inspection at the junior high in your town yesterday."

The more dramatic introduction (which Andrew Dlugan uses) will grab the audience's attention much better.

It is said that Jane Goodall, the naturalist, opened all her presentations with a loud chimp scream. What could be more dramatic or riveting?

Work on your opening more than the rest of your presentation. Memorize your opening. Use strong verbs, and a tight sentence structure. Make it powerful. If you begin with a story, then be sure it is an engaging story with a powerful point. Study story structure to be sure you have all the elements of a good story in yours.

The opening is not another speech. One pastor spends so much time on setting up his sermon that he then rushes through his points. Time yourself. The opening is to set the presentation up and tell them how you are going to help them.

Never tell jokes. Your audience has probably already heard the joke and you probably can't tell it well either. Stay away from jokes. And just to be clear, never ever tell a joke by inserting real people into the joke as if it really happened. More than half your audience will already know the joke and you will lose all credibility with them by telling it as if it is a true story.

The opening should introduce the topic, the problem you are going to help the audience solve, or the truth you will teach. If you use a story or quote opening, then be sure it has a point and that the point is made clearly. The opening must draw your audience to you. Grab them from the first word, and they will stay with you to the end. Memorize your opening. Use strong verbs and a tight sentence structure. Make it powerful. Practice your opening. Stand up and speak the whole opening aloud.

Make them sit on the edge of their seats not settle back and expect to be bored.

Practice

1. Listen for the opening lines in the next presentations you hear. What worked? What didn't work?

2. Review one of your recent presentations. What was the opening line? How could you improve it with one of the techniques listed in this chapter?

3. Read the following first lines from literature. Notice how they intrigue and capture your curiosity. How could you use one of these quotes or a derivation of one of these quotes, to begin your next presentation?

    ▪ "It was a bright cold day in April, and the clocks were striking thirteen." –George Orwell, *1984*

    ▪ "In a hole in the ground there lived a hobbit." – J.R.R. Tolkien, *The Hobbit*

    ▪ "There is no lake at Camp Green Lake." –Louis Sachar, *Holes*

- "It's funny how one summer can change everything." –Sarah Dessen, *That Summer*

- "This morning, my mother didn't get out of bed." –Melina Marchetta, *Saving Francesca*

- "The great fish moved silently through the night water." –Peter Benchley, *Jaws*

Chapter 10
Closings

Instead of firing off a perfunctory "thank you," consider launching fireworks of final passionate thoughts from the podium.

--Peter Jeff

The audience will remember the first and last words you say. Just as the opening draws the audience in and connects them with you and launches the audience into your world, the closing is a summary, a review, an opportunity to stress the importance of your points, and it often calls for a commitment or presents a challenge. The closing will leave the audience satisfied.

Notice how Jesus closed a presentation.

> So in everything, do to others what you would have them do to you, for this sums up the Law and the Prophets (Matthew 7:12).

A well-constructed, powerful sentence will bring the message to the final climax and resolution. A strong closing will bring the audience to a moment of commitment or action. If you do the closing correctly, then the audience will leave with renewed enthusiasm and changed lives. Their future decisions and actions will be changed for the better because of your presentation. They will begin to use a budget to manage their finances, for example, or commit to witnessing about their faith to the next ten people they meet.

Good closings summarize and wrap up. There are numerous ways to close, including giving a summary, repeating the outline or the action points, using a poem or a quote, or telling a story.

Give a Summary

Craft a strong sentence or paragraph which summarizes the important points of your message and asks for action from your hearers. In my presentations about women's friendships, I speak about how the luscious qualities of chocolate compare to the luscious qualities of friendship. My last line is, "So from now on, let chocolate be your cue for great friendships." This statement wraps up the discussion about how forgiveness is as luxurious as Godiva chocolate or how loyalty is like a meringue on a chocolate pie. (It covers everything.) Throughout the presentation, I know exactly what my closing line is going to be so I never stumble to wrap things up.

If your presentation has been a discussion of many facts or factors, then pull it all together in the closing so that your audience will see how these varied facts fit into your main premise. Doing a wrap-up is like a short summary.

Repeat the Outline

A great way to end the presentation is to repeat the points of the outline and summarize or challenge your audience with the changes you want them to make. If you have used action points in the message, then repeat them. "Today, do this. Tomorrow, do this." If your outline is sentences or verbs, repeat the outline and add a closing challenge.

> "God answers personal, peaceful, persistent prayers. Will you begin to pray today?"
>
> "We've seen how God is able, available, and anxious to help us in troubled times. What will you do the next time you face a problem?

Use a Poem or Quote or Prayer

A poem that fits the message of your presentation will evoke an emotional response from your hearers, as long as you speak it well using proper inflection in your voice. A well-crafted quote will help the audience see your point in one more way.

If you want to pray at the end, say, "I'd like to pray for you, and then I have one more thing to tell you." Using a sentence like this will prevent an awkward moment at the end of your prayer when the audience doesn't know if you are finished and whether or not they should applaud. You tell them something is coming after the prayer, then you pray. Then you make your last statement before leaving the stage. Ending in this way helps the audience feel the ending in case they want to applaud and eliminates any awkward moments after the prayer.

Memorize Your Closing

Whatever you intend to do at the end should be so clear in your mind that you can go there from any point in your message. You never know what might happen while you are speaking. Some technical disaster, some emergency, or some other interruption might get you off your outline and the points you intended to cover. But if you know your ending, nothing can get you so distracted that you will forget how to end.

Know your beginning line and you'll always be able to start, even if the size of the crowd or the bright lights make you nervous. Know your ending lines and you can always get to the end no matter what happens during the presentation, or what you may have had to leave out in the middle of it.

If your ending repeats a line or comment from your opening, your presentation will make a complete circle. Repeat the question you started your presentation with or refer to the story or the statistic from the beginning. Great closings change everything.

Use a Final Story

Recently, I was thrilled to discover that a pastor we had known many years ago was to speak at an event where I would be. I loved this man and his preaching for many years. When we arrived at the venue, I was surprised to see how much he had aged. Funny how we never think we have aged but notice it in others. I wondered if the pastor would still have the same fire and vigor and dynamic delivery of his younger years. I didn't need to worry because even though he was not as steady on his feet as when he was younger, when he stepped to the podium, he was incredible. He began with startling statistics, which he quoted without notes. His percentages and facts didn't seem stale or dry because he related each one to our current situation in America. He spoke with power and wisdom and humor.

His message was a call to America to come back to the principles of our founding fathers. As he was ending, he said, "I want us to pray for America."

My first thought was that he had found a good ending. It was appropriate. Prayer is the key to change and transformation. Having the audience pray for the country was a fitting and well-crafted ending.

But then the speaker surprised me. He said, "Before we pray, I want to tell you a story."

> "As a young man, I started in ministry as the musician for a famous evangelist. We traveled around the world with a team and held big stadium evangelistic events. I was a successful musician and I seemed to have a knack for leading praise and worship, but for weeks I struggled because I felt God's call to become a preacher. The team was completing an event in Ireland and leaving for Russia the next day. That night, I told the evangelist about my feelings to become a preacher instead of a singer. The evangelist said, 'If you are going to leave me, do it now!'
>
> "So the team left for Russia, and I stayed in Ireland. I was young, inexperienced, and had no plan and no money.
>
> "One morning the phone rang. It was the pastor of a church in Belfast. He said, 'Laddie, I hear you are going to preach now. So will you come to our church and preach a revival starting next week?'
>
> "I said, 'Yes.'
>
> "But the pastor continued. 'I don't think many people will come. Our people don't like revivals.'
>
> "'Do you have anyone who will meet me at the church on Sunday evening to pray?' I asked.

'Yes, I can get a few.'

"So a group of people met to pray for revival, and we prayed all night and into Monday morning. When Monday night came, the crowds were so big it was standing room only. People were saved and lives were changed, and the revival lasted for weeks."

After telling this story, the preacher looked at us and said, "A lot of things have happened to me in my life, and I may not be sure of a lot of things, but because of that experience in Ireland, I am sure about the power of prayer. Now, will you come and pray with me for America?"

Yes, we did. Hundreds of us left our seats and knelt at the altar to pray for our country.

The impact of his closing was phenomenal. The first closing that I thought he was making was appropriate and made the point. The story closing was remarkable and memorable and made us understand the power of prayer. What a difference!

Closings Matter

Your closing statement or story will be the challenge or encouragement your audience needs. Choose a technique and consider your objective. What challenge or hope do you want to leave with your group? Craft the ending well.

Practice

1. Using one of the openings you crafted in the previous chapter, write a closing that refers (circles back) to that opening.

2. Review your preparation for the next presentation you will give. Write one strong sentence that wraps it up and brings it all together. Memorize that sentence.

3. How did the pastor's story about his experience in Ireland change your mind or give you encouragement about closing well?

Chapter 11
Add a Dose of Humor

A day without sunshine is like, you know, night.

–Steve Martin

No one can teach you to be funny, but you can add wit and winsomeness to your presentations. And getting people to laugh is easier than you may think it is. Since you now know that stories and examples are important to your presentation, you can add humor to your stories. Humor added to any story teaches truth in a fresh, new, and viable way. Humor relaxes an audience and gives them permission to enjoy what you have to say. Humor opens the mind of the audience in a way no other technique can do. Humor creates rapport.

Dispel the Lie

Let's begin by debunking the lie within you that says, *I'm not funny*. If you can laugh, then you can be funny. Finding humor for your presentation is a matter of perspective. What is your own personal sense of humor? What kinds of things are humorous to you? Chances are, the things you find funny will be funny to others. Craig Valentine said, "Don't add humor to your speech, uncover humor within it." As you practice, watch for opportunities to add wit and sparkle to your presentation.

Practice becoming aware of the humor around you. Watch for humor and absurdity in your daily life, and you will be surprised how much there is and where you find it. Sometimes the most heart-wrenching places can have the most humorous elements. My friend's late father-in-law had to be moved to the dementia unit of a local nursing home. Her biweekly visits left her and her husband emotionally exhausted and often in tears, but the unit is also the source of many humorous memories. One time a female patient, in a burst of joyful exuberance, disrobed at the lunch table. Another patient insisted on having my friend carry imaginary packages across the room, and another day the same patient asked her to marry him. Laughter and tears are closely related.

Everyone does something ridiculous now and then. Pay attention to the really stupid things you and others do. Another friend of mine had just finished sweeping her walk, so she carried the broom with her to the mailbox. On her way back from the mailbox, she suddenly spied some leaves under a bush and decided to use her broom to dislodge them. One task led to another and the next thing you know, she was sweeping her yard with the broom.

Practice looking at the world the way children do. They say and do some of the funniest things. Be curious and open. Live "in the mood" to have fun.

Keep your notebook handy to record those humorous moments. Then connect the humor to your topic. Never tell jokes; you don't need them. Your life is funnier than any joke. In my notebook, I've recorded funny things that I've seen on signs; hilarious things the children in my life have said and done; and the silly antics I've observed at sporting events, the local mall, and church. Keep your eyes and ears open and your pen ready. You'll have more material than you can use.

Here is a sign we saw on a country road in Kentucky.

Private Sign - Do Not Read

A sign like this is priceless. A joke is never as funny as reality.

Surprise Your Audience

What makes something funny? Ken Davis says humor has three elements: surprise, exaggeration, and discovered truth. When you want to tell a funny story, you want to surprise your audience. You don't want them to know what is coming. Surprise your audience by putting down a verbal rug, convincing them it is safe, then yanking the rug out with the punch line. Exaggerate the elements of the story.

In a story about my grandmother's feather bed, I describe how you sink into the bed so deep that no one can see you. Exaggerated? Yes, but the audience feels the luxury of that soft mattress as I describe it. Then I tell them about the too-short slats that hold the mattress up and how you can't rest because if you snuggle too deep and let your weight fully sink into the bed, you'll dislodge the slats and bed will fall. After you've exaggerated, you then find a way for the audience to discover the truth within the story. In the mattress story, I show how in God's rest we can truly rely on Him. When you do humor well, you will incorporate all three elements.

Understand Them

With humor, as we have seen with other things, you need to know your audience. Different things are funny in different locales. What is humorous in one country or culture may not be funny in another one. What is the culture and the area where you are speaking? What gender is the crowd? Is there any language barrier that would keep them from understanding your humor? Make sure you are conscious of the age, values, styles, and interests of the audience. Then take the risk and add humor to your presentation. The Bible says, "A joyful heart is good medicine" (Proverbs 17:22). So don't be boring and lifeless; insert your personality and include wit and winsomeness and humor.

Learn about Humor

Read about comedy and improve your abilities. Analyze those people you think are funny and why what they do works for them. Then think about yourself, and determine what works for you. There are numerous types of humor. Learn what they are, and see how you can use the techniques in your stories and presentations. Discover how juxtaposition, irony, oxymorons, misdirection, incongruence, and the rule of three can work for you.

My friend, comedian Anita Renfroe, uses the rule of thirds when she says, "When Mama isn't home, dads feed the children things that end in *o*—Cheerios, Raviolios, and dominoes!" The crowd always laughs because they didn't expect the incongruent last item in the list of three.

As I studied humor, I learned about the importance of using the right word. Humorists know from experience that hard consonants are funnier than soft consonants, so change words to add these hard sounds. *Carrot* instead of *apple*. *Cottage* instead of *home*.

Remember Seven Quick Tips

1. Learn the value of a pause for humorous effect. Often it is what you don't say or the quiet moment before the punch line that makes the humor successful. This is called timing.

2. Learn from comedians and other speakers who are funny, but don't copy them or try to retell their jokes. Learn the

techniques that work such as looks, pauses, and body language. Watch the video of me telling about the name my grandchildren gave me. Notice the pause and facial expressions just as I confirm the actual name.

You need to work within your own style, personality, and demeanor. Be yourself, and use what works with your skills and strengths. Notice when people laugh. You'll discover that some things you didn't mean to be humorous will tickle your audience.

I teach a class on healthy eating. One night I proudly mentioned that my husband and I had resisted temptation to stop at a favorite barbecue restaurant and went home to eat a taco salad. Later, when we calculated the calories, we discovered that our taco salad had a whopping 900 calories. The class laughed with me over our mishap, and I expected that. What I didn't expect was the number of times I could work in the words *taco salad* into the rest of my talk and get an instant laugh from the group.

3. Try to work in something humorous or light-hearted every five to seven minutes of your presentation.

4. The dangers of humor come when we give the secret (the punch line) away before the perfect moment in the story or when we set the story up wrong. Never say, "Oh, you're going to love this one," or, "I'm going to tell you a funny story." These sentences throw up a red flag to your audience who close their minds and think, *You can't make me laugh.*

5. If a story or funny line has any appearance of being inappropriate, leave it out.

6. Give your audience permission to laugh especially after a punch line that might seem insulting. One of my favorite stories is about having my glamour shot made. After

the elaborate set-up of how wonderful I looked in these photographs, I deliver the punch line, "My husband said, 'These are beautiful, who is it?'" The audience howls if I give them permission. From my facial expression, they know I laughed too.

7. Pause after the humorous line to allow your audience to laugh. But don't laugh at your own humor. If you get tickled, smile, then drop the microphone by your side so they won't hear you chuckle. If the humor fails, say something that rescues you. "Some of you will get that one on the way home." "Sorry, I'm from Texas." Famous comedians have planned lines or stances that save the day for them when the audience doesn't laugh. Johnny Carson's line was, "Some of these I just do for me." Milton Berle folded his arms and sighed an exasperated, "Well." Lucille Ball crossed her eyes and made a face.

Set the Mood for Humor

Use your opening as an opportunity to let your audience know you are there to spread joy. Set the tone for humor by creating a fun and funny atmosphere when you begin your presentation. Come on to the stage smiling. If you love speaking, notify your face. Your body language and facial expressions will tell the audience that they are going to enjoy their time with you. One speaker friend, who is a large person, always wears outrageous colors or outfits for her humorous presentations. She's not quite dressed like a clown, but when the audience sees a large person wearing solid bright orange walking on stage, they know either the person is a comedienne or an escaped convict.

You can even warm up your audience *before* you set foot on stage. At some events, especially if I am to speak several times, I will start a slide show before I come on stage. One of the slide shows is a collection of outrageous high-heeled shoes – everything from shoes that look like animals to high-heeled scuba flippers. When I come on stage after that slide show, the audience is ready to have fun. I also have a slide show called, "Why Husbands Shouldn't Babysit." It is a collection of fun photos of children who are covered in suds or have marked on each other with markers or who are eating from the dog's bowl. The slide show is so funny, and every woman in attendance totally gets it. Some even call home to make sure all is well.

When you set the tone for fun, the audience will anticipate your humor. Use video bloopers, funny stories, self-depreciation, clips, or even quotes from Will Rogers or Yogi Berra. Make a collection that you can use to set the atmosphere before your speak.

Know the Punch Line

The key to good humor is practice, practice, practice. Try it out. Tune it up, and then try again. Read funny things; watch funny people; learn the techniques of humor, especially the technique of the pause, and apply these techniques to your personality and style.

Practice

1. Make a list of five things that you think are funny. Consider how you could use one in your next presentation.

2. Watch old TV sitcoms such as *I Love Lucy*. Make a list of comic techniques she uses. How can you use one of them in your next presentation?

Chapter 12
Voice

The exhilarating ripple of her voice was
a wild tonic in the rain.

—F. Scott Fitzgerald, *The Great Gatsby*

Speak in a clear, strong voice so that the audience doesn't miss one word. Getting the most out of your voice may require some work and some practice, but the results are worth it. You will keep your audience's attention, your habits won't annoy them, and your talk will have energy that captivates. The keys to good voice use are volume, pitch, and pace. Listen to yourself in a recorded presentation. Are your words and sentences too fast? Are you too slow? Work on getting a varied pace, and never speak so fast the audience can't understand your words.

Project Your Words

Most speakers aren't loud enough even with a microphone. Don't gulp your words. Some speakers tend to absorb the sounds of their voice into the throat. This keeps the tone muted and gives the effect of swallowing the words. Practice pushing the words out of the front of your mouth so that each word is clearly projected. Ask a friend to help you as you try this experiment. Go into an auditorium-sized room and stand on the stage with no microphone. Ask your friend to go to the back of the room. Speak so that your friend can clearly understand and hear every word. Practice speaking in that tone.

Vary Your Volume

We all have three volume levels: normal, minimum, and maximum. A normal tone is the loudness of your voice when you speak in a conversational tone. Softer than that normal tone is your minimum voice, the softest you can speak and still be heard. Louder than that normal tone is your maximum voice, the loudest you can speak without shouting. You should use all three of these tones in your presentations. Practice out loud to determine what each of the three levels feels like. Then use them appropriately throughout your presentation. Levels of volume bring texture to your presentations.

Learn to Breathe

Support your voice and your words with plenty of air. Inhaling without raising your shoulders will fill your diaphragm. Put your hands on each side of your waist and see if you can feel your diaphragm (just below your rib cage) expanding. Watch yourself in a mirror to be sure you don't raise your shoulders. If you have trouble understanding how to support your voice with your breath, talk to a trained musician. The person who sings in your church has studied and uses good breathing techniques and can help you add power to your voice. If you want to experience how correct breathing feels, lie down on your back on a piano bench or similar hard surface. Then breathe deeply—you will naturally use your diaphragm in this position. When you fill your diaphragm, your voice will take on a deeper, richer quality.

Before a presentation, warm up – much like singers do prior to a concert. Memorize a few tongue twister lines and repeat them out loud to warm up your voice.

You need power behind your words—even your softest voice must be filled with energy and strength.

Forget Filler Words

As you speak, watch for filler words. *And. Ah. Uh. So.* All these words are sounds that come out of your mouth when you are thinking what to say next. It is much better not to make any sound at all than to fill the space with these pesky words.

Some speakers develop a word habit. They use some term

over and over again. The term shows up when the speaker is nervous or trying to fill dead space in the air. Some of those word habits are words like *Amen?* Or *Okay?* These words show up at the end of every sentence, and serve only to annoy the audience. Speakers are often unaware that they have said them.

Once I was coaching a client, and my friend and fellow speaker Florence Littauer listened in. Afterwards, she pulled me aside and said, "You said the words *you know* nine times in one minute." I was completely unaware that I ever used that filler phrase. So she gave me a great tip on how to stop using such terms. She said, "Give your brain an assignment: Brain, every time you hear me say those two words, call it to my attention."

I followed her advice and gave my brain that assignment. Now, if I hear those two words come out of my mouth, my brain hears it, and I adjust my words so that the two words won't slip out again.

If you have a habit word, you can stop. Begin by giving your brain an assignment. It is amazing what your brain can do in the background while you are giving a speech.

Use Energy and Rich Tone

Your voice must have energy and richness, or your audience will not stay with you for a full presentation. A high-pitched voice grates on the audience's ears.

Use the breathing techniques mentioned earlier to help give your voice a more rounded quality. Speak from the diaphragm. Let the vowels form in your mouth and project the words out with crisp beginning and ending consonants. Use pauses and timing well. Some points need a short pause to be fully appreciated. Punch lines and quotations often need a pause at the end to allow them to fully soak into the minds of your audience. Practice pausing. Be sure the timing of all phrases is clear. Some statements need to be stated fast. Other phrases need to be slowed down.

Take time to visit the http://speaklikeJesus.com website to see these techniques in action:

Practice Speaking Scripture

I believe reading or quoting Scripture is one of the most important things we can do as speakers. Never read a passage unless you have read it out loud many times before you are on stage. Practice the words and the phrases. Be able to pronounce every word clearly without hesitation. Practice reading out loud so that you will read God's Word well.

Perform Your Best

In Christian circles it isn't considered good form to call your presentation, speech, sermon, lesson, or talk a performance, but don't be fooled into thinking it is okay to be mediocre. Your audience is well-acquainted with professional performance in every area of life from TV programs and movies to events at work and the Internet. If your words are poorly put together and you don't have a strong point and an interesting way to present it, then they have no real reason to listen. If you practice and you study the craft of speaking, then you will give your presentation with the skill of a professional performer, and you will have the Holy Spirit to bless and anoint you, and the audience will receive the message.

When Jesus went into the synagogue in Capernaum, He read the Scriptures like the people had never heard them read before; He spoke truth to the people with authority and power, and He left them breathless. You can do the same if you work hard on your voice and the energy and skills you need.

Practice

1. Record your next presentation. Listen for filler words. Give your brain an assignment to stop using these words or phrases.

2. Pick out a poem, narrative, or Scripture passage. Practice reading it aloud using a combination of all three voice levels.

Chapter 13
Body Language, Hand Movements, and Eye Contact

The human body is the best picture of the human soul.

--Ludwig Wittgenstein

The Pharisees brought a woman to Jesus. She had been caught in an adulterous act. Jesus did not condemn her. Instead, He knelt in the sand.

> But Jesus bent down and started to write
> on the ground with his finger (John 8:6b).

Jesus' body language and His dramatic pause at the moment of their furor against the woman said more than any words He might have spoken.

What you say and how you say it is only part of your presentation. A big percentage of what you communicate in your presentation is nonverbal. If you are nervous and pacing or slumped over with bad posture, then you will convey a message that may be different than your words. Your body will give out a stronger message than your voice.

Become Comfortable

One of the most important things you can do is make the audience feel comfortable with you. One of the ways you can help your audience relax and become comfortable with you is to remove any barriers that separate you from them. First, remove the podium if at all possible, or at least spend most of your time in front of it or beside it. Standing behind a podium, especially if it is large, will separate you from those who came to hear you speak. A podium separates you from the audience, and reading your material will bore them. Be so prepared that you need no notes, or at the least one small card with a few prompts.

Stand in a comfortable position. Pacing or rocking annoys your audience who will focus on your movements not on what you say. In contrast, standing too straight and too still will lull your audience into a trance. Find a midway point between slouching and standing stiffly and formally. If your stance is relaxed, easy, composed, and unruffled, then you will invite the audience into your world. They will be able to relax, knowing they are in good hands and can trust you.

Move on Purpose

Your audience will appreciate your stage presence if you move with purpose. Walk purposefully to one side of the stage with your eyes directly on someone in the audience. Speak to that side of the room until you have finished that thought or section of your talk. Then, and only then, do you move. You can go back to the center of the stage (your neutral point) or to the other side of the stage. Just be sure you are looking in the direction you are walking and looking directly at someone in the audience on that side of the room. Come to a stop and finish your thought before you move again.

Finding your comfortable neutral position on stage is one key to looking and feeling at ease. And your audience will relax too. Learn to stand still as well as move. When you stand in one place and then move for a reason to another place, your audience won't feel like they are watching a ping-pong match.

Use Meaningful Hand Movements

Find a comfortable, neutral position for your hands. Try to hold them at your sides in a casual way. Do not put them together at your waist and play spider Olympics with your fingers. Instead, place your hands at your sides and then use one or both of them to make a point. Don't illustrate everything you say.

Every movement of your hand should be purposeful. Hand motions will illustrate and support or they will distract and annoy. Purposeful hand movements make your point. Habitual or repetitive hand movements may stop your audience from hearing your point. Don't move half-heartedly as if you are too timid to really express yourself. Sweep your hands when saying "everything" or reach up high when saying, "God in heaven," or fold your arms across your chest when saying, "I refused." When you add these hand gestures, they are powerful, especially if you start and stop the movement with a return of your hands to your neutral position. Purposeful hand movements are much more powerful than fidgety hands going in many directions with no purpose.

Never pump your hands, repeating a movement without purpose. Too many speakers use their hands to emphasize every word in a staccato beat to go with the rhythm of their words. I've noticed this tendency especially if the speaker is using a hand-held microphone. For some reason, such speakers seem compelled to pump the other hand to emphasize their words. These movements tend to mean nothing and become a distraction. It is far better to put your hands to your sides and then use them to make deliberate, meaningful movements that truly illustrate the words you are saying.

Nerves can get the best of anyone, so practice your neutral position. Be conscious that your hands don't contradict your words. Always hold up the proper number of fingers for whatever number you want to illustrate. Your audience will lose confidence in you if you say "three" while holding up only two fingers.

I often tell a favorite story about the lights going off and on during a storm. I hold my hands up high, then I open and close them to illustrate the off-on of the lights. One day, my husband said, "Karen, you need to work on that hand motion. You are closing your fingers when you say the lights went on and opening your fingers when the lights went off." I practiced and practiced until I got the hand motion right. Be sure your hand movements match your words.

Illustrate with Your Whole Body

Your whole body illustrates the message. If you are telling a story with two characters, you can differentiate them by your body language. If one is powerful and confident, then stand tall and speak loudly. If the other is shy or afraid, then show it in your body stance and voice inflection. Using this technique is like being an actor in a one-person show; you need to become each one of the characters in your story. It can take practice to become adept at switching back and forth between characters, but don't give up. Your stories will come alive if you use body language to your advantage.

Never Read Your Manuscript

Reading your presentation is a sure way to kill it. Never ever read your message. If your audience wanted only to hear or read your words, they would have bought your book and not bothered to come to your presentation. Reading your manuscript bores all audiences.

I attended one event along with several thousand people. The speaker was well-known and successful. When he came on stage, he carried a large black three-ring binder, which he placed on the podium. He began to read his message. The words were beautiful and meaningful and he read with great dramatic flair, but he lost the audience because we never saw his face as his head was down. At one point during the reading, he came to a section about witnessing. He read, "We must tell others about the salvation God offers." He looked up at the audience and in a moment of exuberance, he came from behind the podium, jumped down from the stage and approached several people up the aisle saying, "You gotta tell somebody! You gotta tell somebody!" He was enthusiastic and full of life and joy as he got excited about the idea of evangelism.

Then, as if he suddenly realized what he'd done, he straightened up, went back on stage, and began reading again. What a shame! He had wonderful things to say and an amazingly dramatic voice, but his stage presence behind the podium never allowed us in the audience to connect with him or his message.

Make Eye Contact

Your eyes are the windows to your soul. If the audience never sees your eyes, then they will never see the depths of who you are and will never believe your message. You connect to them with your eyes.

Look *at* the audience—not above their heads or at the back of the room. Look directly into the eyes of one audience member at a time. No sweeping the room allowed.

As I watch speakers, eye contact is the one thing that rarely happens. The speaker scans the room right to left but never looks directly at any one person.

If I stand on stage and sweep my eyes over the audience from right to left, then it appears that I am looking at the people. What I'm actually seeing is shapes and colors—a tall outline of a person; green, blue, pink; a shorter outline of a person; gold; a crowded section; yellow; the shape of a beard; yellow, brown; an empty section. I see the room but not any specific individual. Sweeping the audience this way will prevent me from connecting with the audience and they with me.

Looking into the eyes of individuals, one person at a time, is the key to connecting with the audience. Connecting in this way will make your presentations conversational, and people will relate to you and your message.

Research shows that if a speaker looks directly into the eyes of a person in a crowded audience, the people around that person feels the connection too. Each one will feel as if you are talking directly to him or her.

Hold the eye contact until you finish the thought. Look at someone else directly in the eyes, make your point, and finish that thought before you look away. Even if they look away, keep looking at them. Your message will come through strong and clear in a way you never dreamed possible.

Use Your Body, Hands, and Eyes with Purpose

Body and hand language speak loudly. Jesus was an expert in using both. Use both purposefully. Using eye contact well will revolutionize your stage presence and your speaking success.

Practice

1. Stand in front of a mirror and practice standing in a comfortable position with your arms and hands relaxed. Get the feel of this neutral position. Practice using the neutral position in your next presentation.

2. Tell one of your favorite stories and use hand motions that fit the actions. Practice these until you get the movements perfect.

3. Work on knowing (not memorizing) your next presentation so well that you won't need to use notes. Establish the outline in your mind so clearly that you can say it backward and forward.

    Determine what stories and references you will use with each outline point. Firmly get these into your mind and practice giving the presentation without notes or memorization. (Note: Do memorize your opening and closing lines.)

Chapter 14
Take-Away Benefit for the Audience

When you lift yourself up, you let your audience down.

– Craig Valentine

How can you take what people already know and show them how they can reach heights that are bigger, better, and fulfilling beyond their wildest dreams? Giving the audience something to "take away" is the greatest tool we have. Lives will be changed. A take-away is the benefit that the audience will get from putting the points of your talk into practice. What will stay with them after you have left town? And I don't mean items they bought from your table at the back of the room. I am talking about something deeper.

If you are speaking to a business group, then help them see how their product (their widget) can help consumers live a better life. Most corporate marketing departments are savvy enough to articulate how company products can change the lives of users, and you can find that information on their websites. Depending on your audience and the reason you were invited to speak, you will want to think more specifically about how you can help them do something better, faster, or cheaper. Sales teams, for example, frequently need motivation and inspiration, so you will want to give them a take-away that creates those feelings and leaves them with a plan of action for the next time they feel discouraged.

If you are speaking to church leaders, then give them a new vision for their neighborhood. I know of one church who accepted the challenge of a speaker to reach their neighborhood for Christ. They surveyed the homes around the church and learned that the neighborhood had changed dramatically to a new ethnic dynamic. The church changed the style of its worship services, offering music and programs that fit the Latino community. They hired bilingual pastors and held prayer walks throughout the neighborhood. The changes in their neighborhood were dramatic. The message of Jesus was the same—they just used new methods. The speaker had challenged them to change, and they did.

Take-Away Keys

How do you build in a take-away when you prepare to speak? Your work begins with a strong foundation—your content and purpose. To explore potential take-aways, ask yourself these questions:

1. What truth do they know?

2. What truth can I show them?

3. What truth can change their lives?

Then use the Word of God and your personal experiences to answer these questions. What can you say to challenge the audience? What illustrations or stories will stir their hearts, challenge their current actions, and create in them a desire to change? How can your message touch them in a deep place to give them hope for the future?

When I speak on the friendships of women, for example, I like to include the idea of loyalty. I know from experience that the audience hasn't thought deeply about how this attribute is important to friendship. I show them importance of loyalty by using an event from my life. I discovered the value of loyalty, or lack thereof, when someone I thought was my true friend was not loyal to me.

I had helped this person and promoted her to a high position in the organization. Later, when something didn't go well in a project, she didn't take my side. Instead, she joined others in blaming me for the failed project. I was heartbroken and felt deeply betrayed by her lack of loyalty.

So I when I speak about loyalty, I describe how loyalty matters and how a true friend stands by her friend when rumor or circumstances condemn. When (not if) I make a mistake, my true, loyal friends are still my friends. And even when I do wrong, rebel, or fail completely, my loyal friends may confront me privately, but publicly they will stand by me. Non-loyal friends make themselves scarce.

Then, as I talk, I take the concept further with the audience. I challenge the group to make a commitment to each other. I ask them to look at a friend and say aloud, "Dear friend, I'll be loyal to you even if the evidence condemns you." Saying the commitment sentence to each other helps the women in the audience make a life-changing decision to be loyal—a commitment they "take away" with them.

An application is the how-to of real-life, real-time issues and concerns of the audience. The best moment in a presentation is when a listener catches a glimpse of how your point fits into his or her own life. Good speakers watch their audiences then stop to explain things more deeply and more clearly if necessary. If a concept or lesson has some sticky points, then clarify it lucidly. Doing so calms the fears of those in the audience who tend to question everything. For example, if you are teaching about praying big, bold prayers, then take time to explain the difference between having courageous trust for provision and treating God like a candy store.

Give More Than They Expect

Give the audience much more than they paid for and more than they expect. Jesus did this in Luke chapter 5. A man with leprosy approached Jesus. His disease made the man an outcast who was forbidden to associate with people. In his day, there was no cure for leprosy. His situation was hopeless. He came to Jesus looking for answers. No doubt, physical healing was at the top of his wish list.

Jesus did more than comfort the man. He said, "Be clean," and changed the man's life both inside and out forever. He healed the man's disease and He forgave the man's sin, giving him more than he dared dream.

113

The people in our audiences aren't covered in leprosy, but they are in desperate need of inward healing. They are looking for answers. They are asking, "Can you help?"

Our answer should be like Jesus, "I am willing" (John 8:3).

While I don't have a magic wand or the divine healing abilities Jesus had, I can give my audience hope, answers, solutions, encouragement, steps, action points, instructions, and real concrete help.

Once, Jesus was speaking inside a home to an audience packed tightly in every room and overflowing out the door. Some young men lowered their sick friend down to Jesus from the hole they cut into the roof. Jesus said, "Your sins are forgiven." The friends and the crowd didn't expect that! Just like the man with leprosy, these four had brought their friend to be physically healed, but he got more. You and I aren't God; we can't forgive sins. But we can give more than our audience expects, more hope, more inspiration, more instructions to find truth and everlasting healing.

For example, an audience may come expecting to hear a presentation on personality types. The speaker could give a powerful speech on the subject and give the audience what they expected. But if the speaker adds a spiritual component, for example, to the personality facts, then the audience will be given a new understanding. As a speaker, give laughter, stories, facts, but also give the deeper things associated with your topic.

These four friends expected healing for their friend; he got healing *and* salvation. Your audience may come expecting laughter or a good time with friends. Give them what they expect, but add a deeper experience. To do this well requires that you to study hard and be super prepared.

Give More of Yourself

One of the most important aspects of being a speaker is how you relate to the meeting planner and those who have hired you to speak. Having a servant's heart is another way to give more than the group expects. Although you are the speaker, be willing to help in any way you can.

The leader of the synagogue came to Jesus because the man's daughter lay dying at home. He begged Jesus to help. Jesus got up immediately and went with the man. You probably won't be called upon to heal a dying child, but you can move tables and chairs. You can also pray with those who are distressed and hurting. Never lose your desire to help and to help right now.

Practice

1. Examine your presentations. Define the benefit for the audience within the presentation. Write it on a pad of paper. Now list ways that you can emphasize that benefit to your audience through stories, examples, quotes, statistics, or challenges.

2. As you prepare your next presentation, consider what extra benefits and components you can add to make the presentation more beneficial to the audience. Make a list and add each one to the presentation.

3. Look through your presentation. What extra information could your audience use about your topic? Prepare a Tip Sheet for the information. Then prepare a card to give to each person indicating if they will fill out the card, giving their name and email information, you will send the tip sheet. You'll not only give your audience valuable information, you will build your data base.

Chapter 15
Watch the Audience

The better you know the folks to whom you are speaking the more effective your words will be.

– Curtis O. Fletcher

Audiences are perceptive. They know if a speaker is authentic and sincere. How well you know your audience and how well you deal with any distractions or unusual happenings will help them feel relaxed enough to become open to absorbing your message. Handle yourself with grace, with laughter (especially at yourself if the occasion arises), with genuine concern, with wit, and winsomeness.

Never Mind the Distractions

Jesus handled the interruption of the man being lowered into his midst by teaching about the forgiveness of sins. Most of us won't have something as dramatic as a man being lowered from the ceiling while we are speaking, but distractions will occur. Smoke, fire alarms, loud claps of thunder, crying babies, fainting audience members, plus situations we can't even imagine will happen while we are speaking. When they do, our reactions will guide the reaction of the audience and the affect it has on them.

During a recent contemporary church worship music time, a bat began swooping about the large darkened room, throughout the audience, and then up above the stage. As it dive-bombed the worship leader's head, he exclaimed, "What is that?" But he recovered quickly, adding, "Let's rock the bat!" The audience laughed and sang with gusto.

You can't ignore most interruptions, so respond to them with poise and kindness. Your audience will appreciate the relief that acknowledgment brings. If the lapel microphone begins to pop and crack with static, then simply change to a hand-held microphone without any comments, or work a quick reference to it into your presentation: "Trouble is everywhere, even in microphones." If you are calm and composed during a disruption, your audience will be unruffled as well.

If your messages are interesting enough, the audience will listen no matter what happens. Use stories, visuals, and terminology to which they can relate. Make every story compelling enough to cause the audience to want more or to go deeper into your subject, as the disciples did with Jesus, always asking for more. Your audiences will ask for you to return. Individuals will be inspired, for example, to attend Bible study, or get into a Bible reading program on their own. Lives will be changed.

Speak to the Personalities

Your audiences are filled with four different kinds of people. There are the fun-loving, excitable, outgoing, popular sanguine personalities. These people are ready to have fun and will engage with you if you tell stories and add wit and humor to your presentation. You can recognize them by their colorful clothes and their assorted facial expressions as you speak. Be sure you give them colorful descriptions and interesting stories as well as creative, colorful handouts with pictures.

The second group is the organized, controlled, introverted, perfect melancholy personality. This person will pay close attention, will follow your logic, and will want to understand the message more than they want to be entertained. You can recognize them by their neutral clothes and their close attention to your handout. They are the ones with pads and pens, taking notes so they remember what you say. Be sure you speak clearly and carefully, and give all the answers to any fill-in-the-blank sections of your handout.

The third group is the strong, opinionated, hardworking, powerful choleric personality. This person wants to know you are qualified to speak and wants provable facts. Most of all, this personality type wants action steps to take when they go home. Be sure you help them find a way to implement the life-changes you propose.

The fourth group is the hardest to recognize because these people are calm, easygoing, and do not stand out in the crowd. They will listen and even like what you say, but they probably don't want to fill in blanks on a handout. And they don't want to work hard when they leave. Give them permission to relax by giving them small steps they can take, and then help them see the benefits of change.

In every presentation, try to add elements that will resonate with each of the personality types. That way you will give something to everyone. No one will be left out. You might even use a little self-deprecating humor to poke fun at your presentation style and how your personality type delights one portion of your audience while it frustrates or disappoints another type of person. Then you can turn the tables and give another personality type what they want while pointing out that you are simultaneously boring another audience segment.

Connect to Communicate

The individuals in your audience aren't interested in what you have to say as much as they are interested in making a connection with you. If you lose the focus of your message, your presentation will be words alone. If you focus on the audience and what they need and think they need, your presentation will be communication. Consider how the main point of your message will make a difference to the audience next week. Next year. Your audience may not say it aloud, but each one secretly asks the question, "So what?"

Tend Your Sheep

Study your audience, your sheep, as Jesus called them, to determine the issues they face. Be aware of their mood or what may have gone on in their lives earlier in the day. Think not just of surface problems, but also of deeper life issues. What is the culture of this part of the country? What are the trends in this area? What is the economic and social situation? Who *are* these people? Once you've answered these questions, you'll be able to give value and benefit for your audience to enjoy during your talk and to take away with them.

Practice

1. Develop your "go to" line that you will use when a distraction happens in   your next presentation. Practice it before a mirror. Memorize it.

2. Read about The Personalities and learn how you can speak to each personality type in your next presentation. I recommend *Personality Plus* by Florence Littauer.

Chapter 16
Deal with People as Individuals

It is not true that everyone is special. It is true that everyone was once special and still possesses the ability to recover it.

—Criss Jami

Matthew describes how Jesus interacted with people in his gospel account in chapters 8 and 9.

Large crowds followed Jesus.

> When evening came, many who were demon-possessed were brought to him, and he drove out the spirits with a word and healed all the sick (Matthew 8:16).

Even though the crowds were large, Jesus noticed and responded to individuals. A man with leprosy knelt before him. Jesus spoke to him privately, touched him, and made him clean.

> Jesus reached out his hand and touched the man. "I am willing," he said. "Be clean!" Immediately he was cleansed of his leprosy. Then Jesus said to him, "See that you don't tell anyone. But go, show yourself to the priest and offer the gift Moses commanded, as a testimony to them" (Matthew 8:3).

An official asked for healing of a servant. Jesus offered to go to the man's home and then marveled at the man's faith.

> When Jesus had entered Capernaum, a centurion came to him, asking for help. "Lord," he said, "my servant lies at home paralyzed, suffering terribly." Jesus said to him, "Shall I come and heal him?" The centurion replied, "Lord, I do not deserve to have you come under my roof. But just say the word, and my servant will be healed. For I myself am a man under authority, with soldiers under me. I tell this one, 'Go,' and he goes; and that one, 'Come,' and he comes. I say to my servant, 'Do this,' and he does it." When Jesus heard this, he was amazed and said to those following him, "Truly I tell you, I have not found anyone in Israel with such great faith.

Jesus visited Peter's house and ministered to Peter's ailing mother-in-law. The next day two demon-possessed men approached him. He cast out the demons. A paralyzed man came and was healed (see Matthew 8:14-34). Matthew then records his own encounter with Jesus.

> As Jesus went on from there, he saw a man named Matthew sitting at the tax collector's booth. "Follow me," he told him, and Matthew got up and followed him (Matthew 9:9).

Later Jesus was criticized and questioned (see Matthew 9:10-11, 14-16). He taught the truth to all who followed, but he never failed to notice and interact with the individuals. He raised a dead child (Matthew 9:18, 23). He healed an ill woman (Matthew 9:20-22). He gave sight to two blind men (Matthew 9:27-31) and gave speech to a mute man. Though the crowds were huge, he responded and cared for and related with individuals.

Touch Individuals, Not Crowds

Frequently, before or after your presentation, members of the audience will line up or congregate near you, wanting to talk to you. When you speak (especially in Christian events), do your best to respond to these people. Don't try to manage the whole crowd as a unit. If there is a long line, then focus on each person in front of you individually—not the person down the line who might look more interesting or less needy. As you are with one person, don't look over the shoulder of that person at something else. That gives the impression that you would rather be anywhere but there.

Remember the woman who touched Jesus' robe in the crush of a huge crowd in Matthew chapter 9? He stopped to talk to her and to care about her situation. Jesus was willing to see, act, and react to those around him, even when He was on an important mission.

Pay attention by looking each person in the eye. Listen to his or her story. Give each one encouragement and empathy. Pray with the person, if appropriate. Be kind. Pray for God to give you His wise words or show you what to do. Touch their hands. Say healing words.

Deal with each issue that is presented to you one at a time. Don't worry about the person who just left or the person you will talk to next. Make the person in front of you feel as if he or she is the only person in the room. Ask for the person's name, and then use his or her name at least once while talking. Work on your memory skills so you can remember people, names, faces, events, and situations in case you see them later in the day or the event. Then you can respond with grace.

My friend Florence Littauer is a master at making each person feel important. Her eyes never leave your face. She asks great questions and makes you feel she cares. Every person in the crowd who lines up to talk to her leaves the room thinking, *She likes me best!*

Mingle Before and After

Mingle with people and learn something about them. If you do this before your talk, then it will help you know and understand your audience. If you do it after your talk, then it will help you reinforce your take-away for those audience members who are still undecided or confused.

When Jesus left the synagogue, he went to Simon's house and interacted with the family there. Get to know people. If you teach a regular group, then invite them to your home and find out about their family and life. Hospitality like this isn't common in our fast-paced society. When we lived in The Woodlands, Texas, we started a weekly Bible study class that grew from four to about seventy-five people in a short time. I love to cook and entertain, so we decided to host Sunday lunch at our house for class members and others who were part of the church but who we didn't know well. Every Sunday, we had ten to twenty people for lunch.

The reactions we received from people when we called to invite them to lunch were sometimes comical. They would ask, "Why?" because the art of hospitality has been lost in the hurry-up of life. Some people assumed we had ulterior motives and that we were going to push them to join some multi-level, get-rich-quick pyramid scheme, but the rewards of getting to know people were rich and satisfying.

When you speak, do everything you can to get to know the event planners, the team who invited you, and the members of the audience. You are not a hand-shaking politician; you are a servant. You may not be able to heal like Jesus healed Peter's mother-in-law, but you can get involved on a deeper level with people and find out what they are facing. You can care, and you can pray.

When Jesus saw the crowds, he had compassion. I often quiz myself: Do I have compassion on the people in the audience? Do I see them as they really are? People who are loved by God? The crowd may look different from me; they may be different politically or have differences of opinion on social issues such as marriage and family, but I still see them as sheep needing a shepherd. And I love them.

Pay Attention

People need attention, and they need to know that you notice them. Once, when I was the teacher of a large weekly class, I worked hard, making sure things happened in an orderly manner. The class had grown so fast that we hadn't had enough time to organize leadership and enlist others to help with the physical details, such as setting up chairs, preparing handouts, making coffee, and all the other details of getting ready for the class. One morning I was doing all this work.

I had a long list of tasks to complete before the group arrived. But I was interrupted by a woman coming into the room, sobbing.

"What's wrong?" I asked.

"Are you mad at me?" She said.

I put my arms around her shoulder. "Of course not. Why would you think I'm mad at you?"

"You just went past me without even speaking to me."

I was stunned. In my focus on completing my checklist, I had rushed down the hallway past her. I hadn't even seen her. She felt completely ignored, with good reason.

Jesus was never too busy or preoccupied for individuals. In the middle of a crowd, he stopped to talk to a man who was a public outcast. I was focused on a good thing, (getting the classroom and materials ready), but I failed to minister to one of the folks I was teaching. Be willing to see and reach out to those around you even when you are on an important mission. You may need to get your microphone on or talk to the event planner about the lighting, but as important as your mission may be, the people are more important.

Maintain a Ministry Mindset

Look around. See the people at the event. Care about each one. Go to the event early to set up microphones and stage and lighting. Prepare so well in advance that you don't need to make any last-minute changes to your notes. Ask the event planner for a schedule with starting and ending times, so you can plan time to mingle with the crowd.

Jesus was never too busy—even while He was hanging on the cross in pain and misery, dying, with the weight of world's sin on His shoulders. He heard the thief cry out and responded to him.

Practice

1. Ask the event planner for your next event about ways that he or she can help you connect and mingle with the audience.

2. Bring an assistant to handle your back-of-the room book table so you will be free to actively mix and associate with the audience.

Chapter 17
Grow a Platform

Disengage my self-worth from my itinerary.

– McNair Wilson

Gaining a bigger audience and becoming more well-known is not for your own personal recognition. The more people you speak to the more you will be able to accomplish what God has called you to do.

Jesus went where the people were, and He spoke when given the opportunity, according to Luke 4:31.

> Then he went down to Capernaum, a town in Galilee, and on the Sabbath he taught the people. They were amazed at his teaching, because his words had authority.

He taught in the synagogue on numerous Sabbaths. You should also take any and every opportunity to speak to large groups or small. Jesus traveled through towns, villages, synagogues.

He went to Jerusalem, the *in* town, and Samaria, the *loser* town. Go where you are invited. Every opportunity to speak is an opportunity for you to grow as a person and improve your speaking skills. I wan to use the gifts God had given me. When you do the same, you'll be surprised how He will build your platform.

When I first began speaking, the opportunities were few and far between, and I promised God I wouldn't say no to any opportunity to speak. So, today, I do my best to go wherever the opportunity presents itself, and I try to work out the details if at all possible. Finding your sweet spot and operating within the boundaries of that special connection that you alone can have with an audience is the mark of true success when speaking, not large crowds or large fees.

Large or small crowds, big honorarium or not, I try to go wherever and whenever I am asked. I am willing to teach or speak or pray or work. Are you?

Make the Effort

Building a platform takes effort. Your audiences will grow if you care about the individuals in the audience and if you give well-prepared, value-added presentations. Jesus reached out and touched a man— not for show or fame but to truly help the man.

> And it happened when He was in a certain city, that behold, a man who was full of leprosy saw Jesus; and he fell on his face and implored Him, saying, "Lord, if You are willing, You can make me clean." Then He put out His hand and touched him, saying, "I am willing; be cleansed" (Luke 5:12-13a NKJV).

What you do for the good of individuals, no matter how small or how few people see it, will pay off by expanding your success with larger and larger groups. As you help the people God brings to you, He will give you the size groups that are best for your skills at that time.

Join In

At most events, I try to participate in whatever the group is doing. If they are having a style show or doing a mix-and-mingle activity or participating in small groups, I join in the fun. When I attend a small group, the attendees feel as if they have made a new friend in me.

I also like to look for people I can encourage. Spotting hidden talent is like finding buried treasure. Because I coach speakers, I am always on the lookout for people who seem to have a knack or gift for speaking. I often see someone who has great potential speak briefly to the group. At one event, I listened intently as one of the women gave a short presentation. She was a natural and had the audience's rapt attention. Later that evening, I pulled her aside and quietly told her that I saw something special in her abilities and that I thought she should pursue a speaking career. She was so moved that I singled her out. She and I have stayed in touch for several years, and I've loved following her progress as she follows God's calling. I don't pass out these kinds of compliments casually, and I didn't speak to her publicly for show, but I did encourage her so that she may make a kingdom difference as she follows her dream. Sometimes all it takes to change a person's life is one well-timed compliment.

Stay Humble

No one likes to be around people who continually talk about themselves and brag about their house, car, kids, money, skills, or spiritual gifts. Jesus never boasted about himself. In Matthew 8:1-4, Jesus healed a leper and told the man to be quiet. In Mark 1:34, He didn't allow the demons to speak aloud about who He was; He commanded them to be quiet. In Luke 5:13, Jesus reached out and touched a man—not to create a scene or for acclaim, but to help the man. No matter the size of your platform, do the ministry associated with being "the speaker" in as private a way as you can.

When Jesus told the healed leper not to tell others but to go to the priest and offer a sacrifice, He was helping the man change his life. He was saying, in effect, "God changed your life. Now don't glorify what happened, glorify God." Jesus wanted the focus to be on ministry not accolades. It should be enough for us to see people changed. We should not want them to point to us to give us fame, recognition, and glory.

Yet Jesus' fame spread. Yours may, too, but don't lose sight of the fact that your ministry is about changing lives not about becoming famous (see Luke 5:15). Don't revel in or repeat any praise you get. Just serve the needs of the people, encourage those God places in your path, and help in any way you can.

Start Small at Home

The best place to start growing your audience is at home, in your town, in the venues that are closest to you. You need a place where you consistently speak, teach, or present. Look for a weekly Bible study group, a home group, or a class of some kind that challenges you to give new, fresh vital information on a consistent schedule. Your skills will grow. Your confidence will soar. Your abilities will shine.

Be ready to speak at any time. Build a repertoire of on-the-spot presentations you can give in one minute or five minutes or ten minutes. Your testimony could be the topic. No matter the length, make sure it has a great opening and closing. Memorize the verses that go with it. And be ready. First Peter 3:15 says, "Always being prepared to make a defense to anyone who asks you for a reason for the hope that is in you." Be ready. You will gain a reputation as an interesting and powerful speaker, a speaker who can present on short notice. You will become a go-to speaker.

As you build these impromptu presentations, include simple, compelling, interesting stories. People in the audience will want you to come to their town or group. Craft the stories well. I have a message on perspective that is built around one story. I can give the message in one minute, three minutes, or thirty minutes, depending on the needs of the event. Audiences appreciate the message because I have used the techniques in this book to craft an effective opening, tell a perfectly formed story, and conclude with a well-planned and challenging ending.

When an emcee or program director says, "We'd love to have you say a few words today," I ask how many minutes I have. Then I tell the story and the points in exactly that time. The program director appreciates and remembers how professionally I handled the short notice and the time allotted. The audience enjoys and learns from the well-designed words I speak. Members of the audience go back and tell their program directors at home, and I receive more invitations to speak. Your platform grows when you give value.

Build an Internet and Print Presence

As your ministry grows, you will want to create a website that is easy to navigate and looks professional. Make your speaker page inviting. The website should tell event planners what you will do for them and how you will help them be a success. Write a short biography about yourself, starting with today and working backwards. Don't start with where you were born and then give a blow-by-blow detail of your life. Only include things in your bio that are relevant to your speaking career.

Prepare printed materials too. These materials should reflect who you are and what you have to offer. To be most useful, your printed materials must contain the following:

- Your name (You'd be surprised how many forget to include their name.)

- Your contact information (I recommend obtaining a post office box, rather than giving out your street address.)

- A short bio

- Some personal tidbit of information, so people can relate to you

- Information on some of the topics you speak about. Give the topic a clever title. Write a short paragraph with three elements. First, create a hook sentence to interest the person in the topic. Second, write a sentence or two about the content of the presentation. Third, end with a line or two about the take-away, or the benefit, for the audience.

The look of your printed materials and your website should reflect you, your personality, and type of presentations you give. Are you delicate and flowery? Are you sophisticated and modern? Are you all business and no fluff? Make sure your colors, fonts, graphic design, and overall feel of your promotional material reflect who you are.

Market and Promote for More

Want to know the top eight ways to get more speaking engagements? A speaker friend and I did an unscientific survey of our past year's speaking appointments—more than 100 events. These are the top eight ways we got these jobs:

1. Postcards

2. Word of mouth

3. Spin-off events

4. Speaking for free or low fee

5. Friends

6. Speaker to speaker

7. Speaker bureaus

8. National conventions

Send postcards to targeted churches, businesses, and organizations not a general zip code mailing. Get the name of the person in charge of event planning, and follow up with a phone call. Be sure your postcard tells event planners what you will do for them, how they will benefit, how you will make their job easier, and how you will make them a more successful event planner.

Word of mouth and spin-off events happen when you do so well at one speaking event that people can't wait to tell their friends or invite you to their next event. Such enthusiasts often create new events just so they can invite you again.

Speaking at free or low-fee events gives you opportunity to practice and gets you recognition. Consider business groups, service clubs, professional organizations, health groups, women's clubs,

MOPS, and education and parenting groups. All these groups are looking for speakers. The more you speak, the more your name will become associated with the experts in your field.

Friends and other speakers who refer you are the best promotion for your career. One sanguine lady with friends in many places heard me speak and enthusiastically recommended me to others; she has been instrumental in booking dozens of additional events. Join speaker bureaus if they fit your needs, and attend national conventions of church or industry groups to keep your name in the forefront.

Online Value

Systematically set out to promote your speaking career. Use Twitter, Facebook, blogs, websites, and other online sites to make your name well known. Give out valuable information. Provide tips and guide sheets and advice and instructions that will help people. When you post online and give value, your name becomes synonymous with your subject and if you do it well, you will become one of the go-to experts in your field. The reality of the Internet is that people search it for information. They do not want to be given a sales pitch, nor do they want to hear all about you. They are interested in what information and help you can provide to them. They will come back to your blog or follow you on Twitter or Facebook if you give out value. If you are only promoting yourself, they will not pay attention.

Collect the names and email addresses of everyone who attends your presentations. Offer something of value to everyone who is willing to give you his or her email. One friend offers a tip sheet to be sent out by email to all who sign up. Another speaker asks attendees to sign up for the newsletter she emails once per quarter. Another speaker collects names and email addresses and has a drawing for a door prize at the event.

Marketing yourself and building a platform are part of speaking. Decide how you will make your name known, and pursue the online and printed avenues that will get it done.

Practice

1. If you haven't already signed up for Facebook and Twitter, do it immediately. Use Tweetdeck or Hootsuite to set up regular posts to the Internet.

2. Meet with a designer to develop a website and printed material that fits your personality, your ministry materials, and your message.

3. Consider starting a blog or a newsletter to reach potential speaking and or writing clients.

4. Make a form that will enable you to gather email addresses for everyone in your audiences. Have it printed and ready for your next event.

Chapter 18
Build A Team

Light is the task where many share the toil.

--Homer

Jesus began calling His disciples (see Matthew 4:18). He needed a team to minister with Him and to take the reins of the ministry when Jesus returned to heaven. He asked these men to follow Him. He told them what was in it for them with an inspiring message. *Follow me and change the world.*

You should pick a team to help you. You cannot do alone what you must do. Choose reliable people and then share your vision in such an inspiring way that they will give you the much-needed help you crave.

Pray First then Pour Into Your Team

Jesus chose His team after spending all night in prayer (see Luke 6:13). They were an unlikely crew. He challenged them. He cared about them.

Jesus not only loved the crowds, He poured himself into His team. He counseled them privately. He loved them deeply. Jesus taught His team. Read the mysterious contracts in the beatitudes and see how deeply He taught them. They traveled with Him and saw all the miracles and heard His teaching, but they still wondered who He was and they lived in fear. In Mark 4:40, Jesus asked, "Why are you so afraid?" and then, "Do you still have no faith?" He had great expectations for them and wanted them to have courageous faith. As the leader, you should give your team lots to think about and cast a new vision and a higher standard to live by.

The twelve men that Jesus chose were fully trained and He changed their lives to a new level. The soldiers who are chosen to guard the Tomb of the Unknown Soldier at the National Cemetery in Arlington, Virginia, are chosen from a division of the Army's 3rd Infantry regiment's "The Old Guard." They have guarded the tomb 24 hours a day, 365 days a year since 1930. These sentinels are trained in all the protocol associated with the ceremonies and tradition surrounding the tomb set high on a hill overlooking the Capitol. But the training these soldiers receive is deeper and the commitment they make is profound. These soldiers make a two-year commitment to guard the tomb and live in a special barracks, and they commit to drink no alcohol on or off duty for the rest of their lives. Being part of this special group is life-changing.

Consider how you will influence those closest to you – your ministry team. Give your team the opportunity to make forever changes through teaching and mentoring.

Time Together

Jesus spent quality and quantity time with His team. He took the disciples up a mountain for a time to reflect, plan, and dream. It is your responsibility to teach your team and not simply to expect them to do what you want without a clue from you. Model mentoring to them and show them your best. Help each one work inside their personality. Teach them what you have learned. Coach them to write, to speak, to preach, to teach, to serve. Leave a legacy of people. If you have followers, give them jobs. Send them out to do the job. Give clear instructions and guidance—where, how, what to do if rejected. Read how Jesus gave clear, careful, powerful instructions to the seventy-two he sent out in Luke 10:1-17. Even the weakest of His group was trained to go out—even Judas Iscariot.

A student is not above his teacher, but everyone who is fully trained will be like his teacher. I can't be Jesus, but I can be like Him and speak like Him and influence others like Him.

Ask these trusted people on your team for council. Does my talk have any shaky theological points? Do I seem or have I said anything that might be insensitive? Is the point of my message clear?

How To Choose Your Team

Choose hardworking, family-oriented people who are willing to invest time in your ministry. Don't pick people who are trying to make a name for themselves and want to ride your coattails.

When choosing a team, don't be afraid of the one no one wants you to choose. Levi was not an automatic choice (see Mark 1:13-15). People didn't like tax collectors. That person who seems like an unlikely choice may be exactly who you need. A strong choleric personality who may be loud and who expresses opinions with too much brass; or a quiet melancholy personality who analyzes the down side of every idea; or the giddy sanguine who seems too flippant; or a quiet, calm phlegmatic personality who seems disinterested may be best for you and your ministry.

Jesus chose Matthew, who was unpopular and not trusted, but he eventually wrote the Gospel of Matthew using Old Testament prophecies and genealogies to prove that Jesus is the long-awaited Jewish Messiah. No one else could have written it in the same way. The other gospel writers show Jesus in a different light. Mark focuses on Jesus as the Son of God and shows His servant heart and deeds. Luke stresses Jesus' humanity and John, His deity. Each person was either one of the original twelve team members or was greatly influenced by one of them. If you train and prepare your ministry team, they will accomplish much more than you ever dreamed.

Who Should You Choose

In her book *Becoming a Woman God can Use*, Judith Couchman lists seven people that we need on our team. I have adjusted Judith's list to include the four personality types you need for each team member. On your team you need:

- A Celebrator – a person who believes in your destiny and applauds the journey. The most likely candidate for this team position is a sanguine personality. Who else celebrates like a sanguine! Be sure you choose one who has enough choleric to stay focused on your ministry.

- An Encourager – a person who will strengthen your spirit. As one of the spiritual gifts, encouragement can come from any of the personalities. A choleric will coach you and assure you that you can do it. A sanguine will be your loudest and most exuberant cheerleader. A melancholy will carefully choose true and helpful words, and a phlegmatic will surprise you with depth and wisdom because when a phlegmatic speaks, he or she always has something worthwhile to say.

- An Admonisher – a person who will notice when you've taken steps down the wrong road and who loves you enough to correct your path. A choleric is a great choice for this job because who else loves to offer correction? But be sure your choleric admonisher has some softness either from his or her secondary personality or a big helping of the spiritual gift of mercy or the fruit of the Spirit kindness.

- A Planner – a person who looks into the future and sees where your ministry might lead; a person who sees the big picture and is willing to help map the future. A melancholy's outstanding organizational skills and thoughtful creative ideas or a phlegmatic with a contemplative thought process make good planners.

- An Intercessor – a person who wages spiritual warfare on your behalf. Any personality type might be an intercessor for your ministry. The phlegmatic and melancholy will not forget to pray, and the choleric and sanguine will pray fervently.

- A Mentor – a person who has traveled the road ahead and will share wisdom. Find a mentor with your same personality type who will help you operate in your personality strengths.

- A Counselor – one who will assist you through personal dilemmas. A phlegmatic or melancholy will listen to your predicaments and help find solutions.

Ask God to bring these team members into your life either by invitation or though divine encounters. With teams members like these, your ministry will grow and blossom, and you will stay on the right path.

Practice

1. Make a list of potential team members. Determine the personality type of each one. Consider the strength and weaknesses of each one and what part they might play in your team.

2. On a 3x5 card, make a list of the types of people you need on your team from this chapter. Carry it with you to review as you meet new people who might be an asset to your team.

Chapter 19
Refuel and Refresh

Life isn't about finding yourself. It's about discovering who God created you to be.

Dr. Catherine Hart Weber

Once, Jesus went to the mountaintop to pray and spent the entire night praying.

> One of those days Jesus went out to a mountainside to pray, and spent the night praying to God (Luke 6:12).

As I develop my speaking and writing skills, I must develop myself. The two are tied together. If I am responsible for the depth of my life, I can allow God to be responsible for the breath of it.

It is critical to take time away to refuel, refresh, and reinvigorate your life and your ministry. In one of the busiest weeks of His life (Luke 4:42), Jesus got up before everyone else to go out to pray. He had been traveling, choosing His disciples, preaching, serving, ministering—imagine how He might have wanted to sleep in to stretch His human body and snuggle down into the covers. *Just a few more ZZZZs.* But He went out to pray before daybreak. A quiet time is important to you. Life seems too busy to have the opportunity to be quiet. A quiet time is important – not for study or work but for prayer and quiet and contemplation.

Another reason you need to stay fueled up with God is that you will have failures and rejections. Jesus did. In Luke 4:29-30, the people drove Him out of town and wanted to kill Him. He slipped past them and went away. Sometimes you won't be accepted. Sometimes the message you planned won't work. I once spoke at a conference with many speakers. My time slot was right after lunch on the third day. Everyone was exhausted and had just eaten a large meal. My allergies were flaring up and I had taken some strong antihistamines and felt numb. On top of all those facts, I was giving a presentation that was new and complicated and I didn't have it as clear in my head as I usually do. It didn't work. I never connected with the group and many of them dozed off. What a miserable time for me. And them.

Sometimes you will face a group that has issues like Jesus did in this story or like I did at a retreat in the mountains of an eastern state. The church was in the midst of a split, and the women were warring. One table laughed through every session enjoying their own little jokes and clique. Another table cried the entire three days. When these kinds of events happen, you need to move on just as Jesus did. By the way, in verse 31, we are told Jesus went to Capernaum and they loved Him! Keep your heart and soul focused on Jesus, and you will survive these tough situations.

A Daily Place

Do you have an isolated place? Do you go there to meet Jesus? Do you pray and read and meditate there?

Find a spot in your home where you can be with Him every day. A room that is calm and restful. A chair that is comfortable. A place to keep your supplies such as pencils, markers, notepads, journals, a Bible to write in, prayer journal, prayers to pray, thoughts to meditate on, and verses to memorize. Go to that isolated place even if you are tired or busy—especially if you are tired or busy. For me, this means getting up before everyone else. I love the quiet and calm of the early morning. I love my favorite chair, and with a beautiful cup filled with fragrant coffee, I say, "Good morning, Lord." He always meets me there. Where is your quiet place? Did you spend time there today?

Pruning

When we built our dream home on some acreage near Montgomery, Texas, we chose the top of a small hill for the house. So the landscape company had to build up the front steps and walkways. They built four levels with flowerbeds on each level. The first spring, I planted Mexican heather in the lowest beds and also a bed of this favorite flowering bush near the house. That winter, we had several ice storms, so when spring came around again, the plants were brown and looked dead, especially on the lower level. I put my clippers almost even with the ground and clipped the brown bushes down to about one-half inch hoping there was still some life under the ground. When I worked my way up the levels to the bed near the house, I saw that because the plants had some protection by the house, the leaves were yellow but not brown, so I only trimmed off the ends as I shaped the plants. In a few weeks, the plants at the bottom were beautiful, dark green leaves and bright purple flowers, but the plants near the house were still a sickly yellow and had no blooms. The difference? Radical pruning!

One of the important principles of the New Testament is the principle of pruning. We need to be pruned. Bad habits need to be identified and cut out. Pain must be resolved. Work on your craft. Watch yourself on video. Listen to yourself on audio. Work on the skills of speaking. Take courses. Read everything. Get a coach. Do whatever you need to do to get better each time you speak. What point or story or example is weak or doesn't really fit? Which point or statistic or quote is so cumbersome that it slows the message down?

Not only must you and I be willing to prune our messages, we must also be willing to be pruned personally. Are you willing to allow someone to critique your messages? Will you gladly ask for advice and cheerfully accept correction from someone you trust?

A Scheduled Time Away

Several times a year, you and I need to get away for a time to renew. Have you ever gone to a silent retreat? It is a remarkable experience. I attended one in San Diego at a monastery high atop a hill overlooking the ocean. We had a teacher who challenged us to spend long periods of time alone with God with no talking, working, or other distractions. Each of those several-hour-long segments of silence was life-changing for me as I learned to listen to God. I attended another silent retreat in Pennsylvania; each person stopped talking at seven in the evening on Friday and didn't speak again until Sunday afternoon. I discovered God has much to say if I will be quiet.

Life coach Jerome Daley encourages us to consider a recurring sabbatical when we regularly schedule time away from our normal schedule, time we can unplug and listen.

> God is the one who established a created order around recurring rhythms, from the daily rotation of the earth to our annual circuit around the sun and every rhythm in between. This pervasive reality begs us to establish our own rhythms of soul care. While there is no one-size-fits-all, consider an approach to rest and Sabbath that looks like this:
>
> 🕐 One hour a day
>
> 🕐 One day a week
>
> 🕐 One (extra) day a month
>
> 🕐 One weekend a quarter
>
> 🕐 One week a year
>
> Don't get confused. This is not vacation; this is soul-cation. What does one do for soul care in times of Sabbath or sabbatical? Here is my recipe: refresh, reflect, and refocus. In that order.[iii]

Have you considered a sabbatical? I think Jerome's suggestion is one we should grasp and implement.

Time every day and recurring time away and alone will help you grow roots. Pray, read, learn, journal, study, grow. Each time you do, you will become more like Jesus.

For more resources including

Your Marketing Style

Build a Message Worksheets

go to http://speaklikeJesus.com

(Endnotes)

[i] K. S. Wuest, Wuest's Word Studies from the Greek New Testament: For the English Reader (Grand Rapids: Eerdmans, 1997), Mk. 1:21-22.

[ii] Mac Davis, "It's Hard to Humble."

[iii] Jerome Daley, "Give Yourself a Break," Coaching the Coach by Georgia Shaffer, Bold Vision Books, 2013, page 272.

About Karen Porter

Author/Speaker

Karen Porter is an international retreat and seminar speaker and a successful businesswoman. She is the author of seven books.

Karen spends most of her time coaching aspiring writers and speakers and training communicators across the globe.

Karen is a frequent guest on regional and national radio and TV programs. She contributes to national magazines such as **Focus on the Family, Discipleship Journal,** and **American Taste**. She has also written curriculum for **Lifeway Resources.**

Business/Professional

Karen served as Vice President of International Marketing of a major food company in Texas for more than 30 years. She traveled around the world and her varied experiences (including dinners with Fidel Castro) contribute to the richness and depth of her writing and speaking.

Karen and her husband, George, own **Bold Vision Books,** a Christian publishing company.

Karen serves on the board of **Classeminars, Inc,** as well as on the national teaching staff. She also serves on the boards of **First Place 4 Health,** one of the nation's top health and nutrition programs, **Fruitful Word Ministries,** and **Right to the Heart Ministries.**

Personal

Karen says her marriage to George is her greatest achievement, but she'd love to talk to you about her five grandchildren! In her spare time, Karen continues her life-long quest to find the perfect purse. Karen is a people person, plain and simple and you will love to laugh with her and maybe even cry a little as she shares her joys and struggles.

Invite Karen Porter to your next event.

Connect with Karen at:

www.karenporter.com
www.speaklikeJesus.com

Email: kaeporter@gmail.com

Follow Karen on twitter and Facebook

Karen Porter
　　　@Karenporter

Made in the USA
San Bernardino, CA
19 August 2014